Balanchine and Me:
Be Relevant, Not Reverent

Peter Martins

Balanchine and Me:
Be Relevant, Not Reverent

Peter Martins

Academica Press
Washington~London

Library of Congress Cataloging-in-Publication Data

Names: Martins, Peter (author)
Title: Balanchine and me : be relevant not reverent | Martins, Peter
Description: Washington : Academica Press, 2024. | Includes references.
Identifiers: LCCN 2024930013 | ISBN 9781680536263 (hardcover) |
9781680536287 (paperback) | 9781680536270 (e-book)

Contents

This book is dedicated to

George Balanchine

and

Darci Kistler (Mr. B's Last Ballerina)

Fig. 1: Photo by Paul Kolnik pictures Darci Kistler and George Balanchine
backstage at New York State Theatre.

Chapter 1:

Introduction

Fig. 2: Portrait of Peter Martins in the 1970's.

When I came to the United States in 1967, American male ballet dancers were trying to evade the old stereotypical cliché, "What were guys doing dancing in tights?" In the 1930s, a number of American dancers disguised themselves as Russian to gain credibility as classical dancers. For example, the American Marcel Le Plat had joined Colonel Wassily de Basil's Ballets Russes as Marc Platoff but became Marc Platt when he later joined the cast of *Oklahoma*. Another example is the satirical "Great Petrov" in the Fred Astaire movie *Shall We Dance*, who is later revealed to be Peter P. Peters. In the 1940s and 1950s, another answer was found in the bright boy, hearty demeanor of athletic dances that sometimes seemed closer to music hall comedy than classical ballet. By the 1960s, an aesthetic emerged that held that dancers had to be strong, that tights were a variety of gym attire, and that the macho guys who danced had to worry about physique and stamina to the detriment of perfect placement and accurate performance of the classical vocabulary.

This somewhat insecure emphasis on "maleness," even in such fine dancers as Edward Villella and Jacques d'Amboise, was what I found when I came to New York. It was difficult for me to understand, given my European background and the pride in dancing I had always felt. Rather than be smothered by an often boisterous personality, my intention was to strip dance down to uncluttered essentials that would convey to the audience the maximum lucidity of the piece. I always felt I could be both a Balanchine dancer and myself with complete integrity, and that there was no conflict between the two. I have tried to steer clear of being a superstar and focused on being the best dancer I could be. Others have said my style and performance are more Platonic than Olympian. I have always been concerned with the idea of dancing, the beauty of the dance forms, especially sensitivity to shape.

From my present vantage point, now that I am in my mid-seventies, I believe that the fullest expression of my personality has been in my choreography. In 1982 Robert Cornfield wrote that he sees my wit in *Calcium Night Light*, my precision of thought in *Sonate di Scarlatti*, my romantic imagination in *Tchaikovsky Symphony No. 1,* and my prankishness and sentimentality in *The Magic Flute*. That is doubtlessly true as it is for the many ballets I have choreographed in the decades since.

None of this, of course, could have happened without George Balanchine, who did so much to help me resolve any potential conflict between personality and meaning in attaining the creation of the fullest possible expression of balletic dance. I remain deeply indebted to and grateful for all this wonderful man gave to me and countless others.

Perhaps the best way to start this story, then, is to go back to the very beginning.

Chapter 2:

Early Years and Edinburgh 1967

Each year, at the end of the Royal Theatre season in Copenhagen, auditions are held for the ballet school. Children, for the most part between the ages of eight and eleven, come to the school for the entrance examination. The audition room is an old ballet studio with worn wooden floors whose walls are lined with portraits of August Bournonville, and in one corner stands a bust of this nineteenth-century ballet master and choreographer who created the Danish ballet style.

In small groups, the children are seated in a row and asked to remove their shoes. The ballet master and some teachers walk slowly down the line, the ballet master sometimes holding a baton. The children raise their feet, and the shape and extent of each arch are scrutinized, the curve of the instep examined. The foot is a clue to potential ability—the children are being examined for a crucial indication of a dancer's physical equipment. When I was a child, in the early 1950s, the Royal Danish Ballet School wanted a small foot with a big arch and a big instep.

Next, the children are asked to stand, and their overall proportions are considered. No low legs (short limbs), no extra-long legs. The teachers are looking for a pleasing appearance, and for the perfectly proportioned. But talent can override all shortcomings (in my case it had to override big feet). The next test is a dance, and the dance is a simple waltz. The students are arranged in a circle, and since most of them have had classes in social dancing, the test is an easy one, but it demonstrates grace and musicality and how the body moves. Intelligence isn't being tested, but it will be demanded later on.

Equipment, proportion, musicality, and intelligence: these make a dancer. (Well, talent and dedication also play a role).

Fig. 3: Peter Martins during his time as a student at Royal Danish Ballet School.

In a country of five million, only about 50 students are accepted. The School's total enrollment is 250. Of these, only a few finish the course, for each year the students are tested, and the unpromising weeded out. A very select number of those who are graduated are asked to join the Royal Danish Ballet. In 1954, when I was eight, I was accepted into the School.

My mother's side of the family had been involved in music and dance for generations. My mother was a pianist who traces this predilection to her own mother, who, unknown to her parents, spent many childhood days with the local Copenhagen circus, learning simple acrobatic feats and entertaining between acts. Her thwarted theatrical ambitions blossomed in her children. My mother's brother, Leif Ornberg, was a leading dancer with the Royal Danish Ballet, and his wife a prima ballerina. Another uncle was a percussionist in the Theatre Orchestra, and a cousin who was in the ballet company was married to a violinist. Another aunt had her own dance academy. Ours was a family steeped in the arts, and my mother saw no reason why her son should not continue the tradition.

Fig. 4: Photo by Rigmor Mydtskov pictures Peter Martins at Royal Danish Ballet School with Instructor and Director Frank Schaufuss, 1958.

My father, an engineer whose designs and ambitions for a native-made Danish automobile came to nothing because of the industry halt caused by World War II, had no interest in dance or in any of the arts for that matter. He and my mother divorced when I was two, and he never exerted any influence on my choice of career.

As it happened, my heritage and family connections were of no help to me when I first attended the Royal Danish Ballet School. In retrospect, they seem to have created problems. My sisters Marianne and Annette auditioned the same day I did and were not accepted for reasons that remain unclear. Some of my relatives felt that there were teachers and dancers who intensely disliked my family, and that we children were being victimized for quarrels that had nothing to do with us. It is likely that my acceptance was based on the School's being short of boys, a problem shared by dance schools all over the world.

At the end of each year, for seven straight years, my mother received a letter from the School authorities: "Peter is possibly talented, maybe he has some aptitude, perhaps some gift, but we have not made a conclusive decision, and we must warn you that we are still watching his progress. So, we leave you with the caution that this next year might be his last at the School."

The school is a full scholarship School, and all my expenses, including dance shoes and class clothes, were covered. Ballet classes were held in the morning; in the afternoon we had our academic subjects, and at the end of the school day were rehearsals for performances – a mix of ballet, opera and drama, all of which used children to fill up the stage.

Figures 5 and 6: Family photos of Peter Martins in Social Dancing Class.

After my parents' divorce, my mother moved with my sisters and me to a small apartment. Being the sole male, I had a room to myself, while my sisters shared one. The 45-minute trip to school involved two street cars, but when the weather was good I would cycle. For lunch, my mother packed open-faced sandwiches of salami, liver pate, thin slabs of chocolate, and banana on dark pumpernickel. After school, I would go home for an early supper, return to the theatre to perform, and then go back home by myself after the performance. Copenhagen was a safe city, and I wasn't afraid of traveling alone.

There was no guarantee of success, however, and my early years at the school were not pleasant for me. I didn't feel liked by the staff and instructors, and I sensed a personal antipathy because of my family. But even at that age, I had enormous pride and would have thought it an unendurable disgrace and, even more, a family dishonor if I had been expelled. No matter how much I loathed the School, I felt I had no choice but to remain and excel. My instructors grudgingly conceded that I had some talent but were skeptical I could develop it fully. This effort forged a quality that turned out to be a strength in later years: a faith in my talent, an assurance that was developed not by constant praise from others but from an inner, self-sustained belief in myself.

From the age of five, I had social dance classes, and I always felt good at it. For five straight years, my partner and I won the silver medal in the Danish National Social Dancing Competition, losing out to the same couple every year for the gold medal. The winning boy was the son of Denmark's leading social dance teacher, and in the sixth year I finally beat him. With that accomplished, I retired from social dancing competitions. Dancing was something I did better than any of my classmates. It was easy (then), and I just did it. I realized afterward that I didn't have to search for an ambition. I would be a dancer and that was fine.

By my early teens, I had become rowdy, quarrelsome, sometimes snotty, and completely undisciplined. Stanley Williams, a principal dancer with the Company, became my teacher when I was twelve. He had been born in England, but his mother was Danish and his family moved to Denmark when he was a child. When a dancer says, "So and so is my teacher," he means this is the one who determined my style, who gave me the clue to the art and my way of performing. This is the teacher who set my goals, who set my standards of movement. It was Stanley who first made me feel the challenge, the potential achievement, and the *importance* of being a dancer.

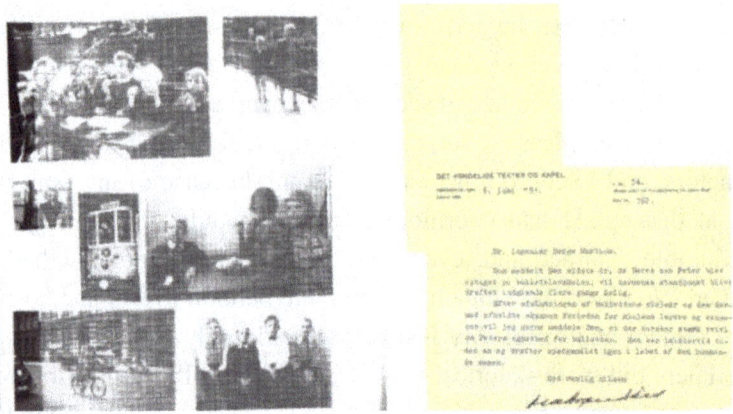

Fig. 7: Letter from the Royal Danish Ballet School relaying a strong "doubt about Peter's suitability for the ballet." See Fig. 7 credits for full translation.

Figures 8 and 9: Photos by Martha Swope picture
Peter Martins with Stanley Williams.

What Stanley taught was not the traditional, Bournonville style of dance, but a way of dancing classical ballet that took account of the present, that was modern in feeling. It was a living method that held the possibility of exploration and extension and variation of the classical technique. What appealed to me about Stanley was his attitude—one of honesty, directness, and lack of fuss. I worked hard under his tutelage. Thanks to him my talent emerged. I graduated and became an apprentice in the Royal Ballet. In 1967 I was promoted to principal dancer, and that spring I was assigned to Balanchine's *Apollo*. Henning Kronstam coached me in the role, and the reviews said I was fair.

That summer, Stanley returned from New York, where he was teaching at the School of American Ballet. We were having dinner at his hotel when a call from Vera Volkova came for me. She had been searching for me everywhere because a small group from the New York City Ballet was supposed to open the day after next in *Apollo* at the Edinburgh Festival, but Jacques d'Amboise had been injured. Balanchine had asked John Taras, one of the Company's ballet masters, to comb Europe for a replacement.

Fig. 10: Peter Martins and Stanley Williams
at SAB studios rehearsing *Flower Festival*.

Taras had flown to Copenhagen hoping to audition me that very night. I replied that it was impossible. Instead, Taras, Volkova, and I met at the theatre the next morning. Taras cabled Balanchine that help was on the way. We flew to Edinburgh later that day, amid a growing chorus of press coverage, and Mr. B watched me go through the ballet without making any major changes, except slight adjustments to the *pas de deux*. The opening was a big success, and my effort was judged heroic. Proud that I had not let anybody down, I arrived at the theatre for another rehearsal the next day.

"Before we begin," Balanchine said, "You know, you do it all wrong." He tore up my performance, but he was very pleasant about it and demonstrated what he meant, even partnering with Suzanne Farrell to show me what he wanted. Suzanne's only comment was, "at least he's tall."

Balanchine told me I was dancing too classically, and I was not giving the role the suggestions of character and imagery he had built into it. I had been trying to make everything look beautiful and grand, but he demanded shapes that looked grotesque but were packed with energy. He was so wonderfully natural. He was an enormously great man. From my first glimpse of him, I knew what dancing was all about. He radiated knowledge and authority. He was never condescending, and he never pretended to know more than he did, yet maybe there wasn't much he didn't know. These were the same qualities that had drawn me to Stanley Williams.

I fell in love with George Balanchine!

On the plane back to Copenhagen, I asked Stanley what I should do next. If Balanchine liked me, Stanley assured me, he would be in touch. What Stanley could assure me of was that Balanchine had been impressed. "You see, I changed everything for him, and he remembered everything."

Back in Copenhagen, my world felt lifeless. But eventually my patience was rewarded: two months later a telegram came. George Balanchine invited me to New York to appear as a guest dancer during the run of *Nutcracker* performances in December.

Fig. 11: Royal Danish Ballet departing for tour,
1965. Martins is pictured on the far left.

Chapter 3:

Coming to New York

I arrived two days before my debut with the New York City Ballet at the New York State Theatre, as it was then known, in December 1967. Dancing the Sugar Plum Fairy's cavalier and partnering with Suzanne Farrell, the critics were welcoming. After two weeks, Balanchine asked me to stay on to learn *Diamonds*, the concluding ballet of a tripartite evening called *Jewels,* and a ballet created especially for Suzanne.

Fig. 12: Photo by Martha Swope pictures Peter Martins
in *Nutcracker* during his early years at New York City Ballet.

This began a tense period with the Royal Ballet in Copenhagen. I returned to Denmark, but when the NYCB spring schedule was finalized, they wanted me to perform *Apollo* and *Diamonds* again, and to partner with Suzanne in Balanchine's setting of Brahms's *Liebeslieder Waltzes*. Jacques d'Amboise had a string of injuries that kept him out—and me in. I was learning ballets overnight and performing them the next day. My performances went well, and Mr. Balanchine finally made me the offer I had dreamed of. Whenever I was free, he wanted me to perform with the Company.

Fig. 13: *Presse Foto* pictures Martins, Inge Olafsen, Anna Laerksen, and Eva Kloborg in *Apollo* at the Royal Danish Ballet.

For the next year and a half, I juggled performing in Copenhagen and New York, to the Danes' increasing annoyance. I applied for a two-year leave of absence, or indefinite leave to Flemming Flindt, the artistic director, who had himself received one years before. "Not possible," he said, "those days are over." In the end I tendered my resignation and told

Fig. 14: Martins in *Diamonds* during his early years
as a dancer at New York City Ballet.

Mr. Balanchine I was free to join his Company as a permanent member. There was nothing easy in any of this. I was leaving my family and the institution that had nurtured me. My relationship with my son Nilas's mother could not be salvaged, but I made a point of spending summers with my son ever since, and experienced the joy of watching his dance career develop successfully here in the States.

For all the difficulties, I had never felt so relieved in my life. I had freed myself of a burden and made a strong commitment to start in a new direction. With my resignation from the Royal Danish Ballet, all should have moved forward smoothly, but it wasn't to be like that.

After arriving in America, when I was roughly 22 years old and had yet to make friends, someone recommended that I go out more to mingle with people. Once I went to a party at a hotel in midtown because I was told I might meet some pretty famous people. I thought to myself, why the hell not? When I arrived, I encountered Faye Dunaway, sitting on the floor smoking a joint, and Tennessee Williams. To my surprise, he asked me to dance. We danced for about two minutes, and I must admit I was very uncomfortable, as he pulled me in quite close. When our dance ended, he was not pleased. As I left, I asked myself how many men could claim they danced with Tennessee Williams. Despite the discomfort in the moment, I still, to this day, find humor and joy in the memory. As life continued in my early years in New York, I began to put myself out there more, making friends in the company. My lonely days of isolating in my apartment began to diminish.

Fig. 15: Photo by Steven Caras pictures
Peter Martins and Suzanne Farrell in *Diamonds*.

The Ballet's 1969 spring gala at the New York State Theatre was the occasion for the premiere of a new ballet by Jerome Robbins called *Dances at a Gathering*. It marked Robbins's return to the Company after a long absence. It was an important night in ballet history, upstaged slightly by Suzanne Farrell. A few days before, Balanchine had fired her and her husband, Paul Meija. Suzanne had demanded that Meija be cast in *Symphony in C*, or they would leave the Company. This left me without the partner I was most at ease with, and without a clear place in the Company.

Chapter 4:

Early Struggles

When I first became a member of the New York City Ballet, Balanchine was not teaching the Company class every day. When he resumed teaching daily, he noticed that I was attending less and less. I learned what I was told to learn but nothing more. In my mind, I was a classically trained, conventional artist, and the classes were unconventional.

The other reason I began avoiding Balanchine's class was that he found me an easy target for ridicule. My attempts to achieve a cool perfection irritated him, and when he imitated my style, he made me look prissy and over-refined. This was devastating, and I felt humiliated. My response was to become even more reserved so that Mr. B and others felt I was distant, even uncommunicative and uninterested, which was completely untrue.

Things came to a head when Balanchine programmed *Theme and Variations* on the last part of Tchaikovsky's *Suite No. 3, in G*. Balanchine created new choreography for it, extending its summation of classical ballet into a dance essay about mood, a dream, with implications of loss and regret, desire and guilt. After the first day of rehearsals Balanchine called me into his office and told me directly what he had been implying in his remarks about my stiffness, lack of expression and general clumsiness in rehearsal. He said I was unusable.

Fig. 16: Photo by Martha Swope pictures Martins dancing *Suite No. 3*.

I was only 23, and patience and tolerance were not my chief virtues. I complained to the Company director, Lincoln Kirstein, who was sympathetic and promised I would soon be featured in a new production, Fokine's *Les Sylphides*, presented under its original title, *Chopiniana*. Here again, Balanchine and I clashed, and I considered leaving the Company and going to the American Ballet Theatre. Instead, after intense consideration, I recommitted to the New York City Ballet and asked Mr. B to clarify my position.

"You see, dear, you don't seem to be interested," he said. "I never see you anywhere, except O'Neal's restaurant. When people show interest, I use them. If they don't, I leave them alone. And you don't show interest."

(Left) Fig. 17: Photo by Martha Swope pictures Martins doing chest pulleys.

Fig. 18: Photo by Martha Swope pictures Martins, Suzanne Farrell,
and Marnee Morris in *Apollo* during his early years as a dancer
at New York City Ballet.

I was shocked. We had been getting the wrong messages, and our misunderstandings had been deepening every day. Rather than coolness and lack of interest, I felt frustration and anger, yes, but also tremendous energy and passion. When I told him this, he responded that, in that case, I had to change my attitude, show him I was willing to work hard, to concentrate and behave maturely. It was now up to me to prove my seriousness and determination. If I succeeded, he'd let me do anything I wanted.

Fig. 19: Photo by Steven Caras pictures Martins in *Apollo* during his later years as a dancer at New York City Ballet.

Mr. B was right, of course, when he noted that he often found me at O'Neal's, rather than in rehearsal rooms. I confess that I had developed an addiction to their famous cheesecake. I would go there daily for a slice. Obviously, I put on weight, which I regrettably noticed in the mirror. It was my first time having love-handles, which I ironically used to tease other male dancers about, by grabbing them. *Apollo*, in which the boy wears very little, soon became a scary ballet to be dancing. I tried desperately to hide it from everybody, until I could get my weight down. I did, thankfully, but I had to give up O'Neal's and its cheesecake.

This was the turning point in my career with the NYCB. The atmosphere altered immediately. No longer did Mr. B disdain to say hello, but instead smiled and welcomed me. And, needless to say, I reciprocated, smiling and bowing at every opportunity. Soon it felt as if we had become friends, if not friendlier.

Ironically enough, after I recommitted to NYCB, Balanchine would often ask me to meet him at the Empire Coffee Shop for lunch. When he asked, of course, it was okay to miss rehearsal. It was his tradition to start with a shot of Aquavit, the famous Danish liquor, followed by a tuna sandwich. We would talk – or rather he would talk and I would listen – about politics, race relations, crime, women, wine, food, and music, but never dance. In other words, we never discussed ballet.

Mr. B was particularly concerned about the spread of communism, which he felt could potentially ruin the world. In regards to race relations, he worried that the history of racism in America would continue to pollute the years to follow. Mr. B was equally concerned about the rising rate of violent crime, which he worried was impossible to halt.

When it came to wine, Balanchine gleefully announced that he had purchased a case of a very rare vintage that would not be drinkable for, in his words, "another 30 years." Of course, he was in his early seventies at that point and would never get the chance to taste it. When it came to women, Mr. B was entirely enamored by a famous Danish actress whose name now escapes me but whom he felt was the most beautiful woman he had ever seen.

Food was perhaps his favorite subject. Balanchine liked to cook, and Swedish meatballs were his specialty. He was adamant that each ingredient be fresh. On one occasion, he introduced me to what he called a "Russian hamburger." He had American hamburger buns on his kitchen counter, along with a huge bowl of caviar. He then proceeded to smear three huge spoonsful of caviar onto the bun. It was the best "hamburger" I had ever had, but of course I was astonished, knowing I was eating roughly – if I were to guess – a three thousand-dollar, Russian burger.

Once, with the NYC Ballet in Copenhagen, Mr. B asked me, "Do you know what my favorite dish in Denmark is? Pea soup."

"My mother makes a delicious pea soup. Let me take you to her house."

We went to her suburban apartment, and he was courtly and impeccably polite when she fed him. "Don't worry, dear," he said as we finished, "I will take care of your son." We walked back down to the taxi, and he said, "Don't tell mother, but that was the worst pea soup I ever had."

I lied to her and said he loved it.

After a meal at home, Balanchine would show his paintings – Bracques, Picassos, Matisses. "Picasso is not that great a painter," he intoned, "Matisse is much better." There was one instance when I was able to get a word in, so I asked him whom he had voted for in the American presidential election. I realized it was probably an inappropriate question, but he readily answered that he had voted for Richard Nixon. "You know why, dear?," he asked me. "He established the National Endowment for the Arts." (Actually, it was Lyndon Johnson, but who was counting?) Mr. B and I may not have spoken much about ballet during those dinners, but art was always at the back of his mind.

Fig. 20: Photo by Steven Caras pictures George Balanchine and Peter Martins at the Russian Tea Room in New York City.

Fig. 21: Self Portrait of Mr. Balanchine gifted to Martins in the 1970's.

George Balanchine

Fig. 22: Portrait of Martins drawn by his mother, placed
alongside a portrait of George Balanchine in family photo album.

Chapter 5:

Growing

In June 1972, the Company staged its Stravinsky Festival, Balanchine's homage to his most celebrated associate, and a tribute to the greatest composer-choreographer partnership of the twentieth century. It was to be a week's worth of ballets, but the highest anticipation, of course, was for Balanchine's new ballets. It was during the making of Stravinsky's *Violin Concerto* that Balanchine first worked with me closely. In rehearsal he was still occasionally testy with me, but occasionally he also showed how impressed he was and, in the process, stretched my abilities as a dancer. *Violin Concerto* was my opportunity to show that I could dance "Balanchine," and I threw myself into the challenge. Once he saw my level of engagement, he gave still more. The experience gave me an incredible high. There is an electric moment when the dancer and choreographer are in synchrony, when the dancer catches the choreographer's intention so easily that they seem to be working totally together.

(Left) Fig. 23: Photo by Martha Swope pictures Martins and Kay Mazzo in *Violin Concerto*.

The result of all this work was a happy surprise. Balanchine had brought me on to discover how I could vary, increase, and extend the reach of the way I danced. In so doing, I lost any fear of failure and was willing to try anything, allowing me to discover my own way of moving. I had found a way of behaving more fully on stage. I was changed as a dancer, for now there was more of me imaginatively in the works. I had discovered how to make dancing a creative act.

Fig. 24: Photo by Carolyn George pictures Martins and Lourdes Lopez in *Violin Concerto*.

•   •   •

When I was 25 years old and a new dancer in the Company, Mr. B came to me and said, "You teach the class."

"You mean at the School."

"No. Company class."

"Are you sure?"

I started with barre for 25 minutes, then moved to the center of the room. Mr. B came in and said, "Can I watch?" I gave the dancers some new step combinations to impress Balanchine. At the end of the class Mr. B beckoned me to his office.

"You know, dear, Terrible!"

"What?"

"That's not ballet class. Don't invent. That's not teaching. That's choreography. Just give them steps and repeat and repeat and repeat. Don't choreograph in class. Choreograph on stage."

I learned at that moment that he was always dead honest.

Fig. 25: Photo by Steven Caras depicts
Martins rehearsing *Sonata di Scarlatti.*

Fig. 26: Photo by Steven Caras pictures Martins teaching students
at the School of American Ballet, including Jock Soto (right).

. . .

Partnering is perhaps the most essential ingredient for both the male and female dancer to succeed. I came out of the Royal Danish Ballet School with a fundamental knowledge of basic partnering skills. I was good. In fact, I was probably the best due to my height, long arms, and large hands. More importantly, however, I loved it. For some reason, partnering gave me more gratification than dancing itself. I cherished the idea of standing behind a ballerina with the intent of making her shine, rather than me.

(Left) Fig. 27: Photo by Steven Caras pictures Martins and Suzanne Farrell in *Tzigane*.

Upon arriving in America, I thought I knew everything about partnering. But I was wrong. George Balanchine showed me what partnering was ultimately about. His ballets were examples of the extent to which partnering could expand and reach new heights. His insight into partnering was, for me, revolutionary.

For instance, Balanchine would often tell me: "Don't just stand behind her, get out of her way." Then he would tell me to come in only if my partner really needed me. He would also often demonstrate himself how to let a ballerina off-balance, before bringing her back to her center. This was not an easy task, but it is one I became, with Mr. B's help, very good at. I discovered myself that if I leaned a girl out, off balance and to the right, I needed to counterbalance the movement with me leaning to the left.

Fig. 28: Martins and Suzanne Farrell in *Chaconne*.

Fig. 29: Photo by Steven Caras pictures
Martins and Suzanne Farrell in *Diamonds*.

Throughout my career as a dancer, I discovered through Balanchine's ballets how to apply that aesthetic to my own choreography. When I began to choreograph, I was obviously fascinated with the challenges that partnering offers a dancer. I thus experimented a great deal with choreographing partnering. Many male dancers were excited to take on those challenges, although some rolled their eyes. Even Jock Soto – a young dancer whom I promoted to Principal at the NYCB, loved to watch dance, and who himself was a natural partner – balked at some of my desires. Nevertheless, he always managed to perform the partnering, often finding solutions to my extreme wishes on his own.

Figures 30 and 31: Photos by Martha Swope picture Balanchine, Martins, and Farrell rehearsing *Chaconne*.

One of the last *pas de deux* I created for the Company, *Infernal Machine*, with music by Christopher Rouse, led many male dancers to avoid dancing, as they all profess it to be too difficult. I, of course, think it's not. Amar Ramasar, for instance, confessed to me that it is the hardest ballet he has ever partnered in. Of course that doesn't give me pleasure, but it speaks to the constant desire I had to explore all partnering possibilities.

Figures 32 and 33: Photos by Martha Swope picture Martins and Darci Kistler in *Histoire du Soldat*.

One of the greatest lessons I learned as a dancer was when performing *Brahms-Schoenberg Second Movement*. I never thought I would be able to master its intricacies, yet Balanchine insisted that I could, and I did. I mastered the technique and even came to enjoy performing it. It was this love of partnering that Mr. B instilled that influenced so much of my own choreography.

Fig. 34: Photo by Carolyn George pictures Martins and Patricia McBride in *Brahms–Schoenberg* Second Movement.

Chapter 6:

Balanchine At Work

There is a common notion that Balanchine was a woman's choreographer. "Ballet is woman," he would say, which eventually became something of a cliché. Yes, Mr. B did like to choreograph for women, because he preferred to look at women, and also because of the added dimension of *pointe* work, but the roles I danced for him all had fascinating challenges and I am very proud of the wonderful parts he created for me. Some of the early great roles I danced include Stravinsky's *Violin Concerto*, Stravinsky's *Duo Concertante*, and Gluck's *Chaconne*. Having said that, the list of Balanchine's female roles is longer.

Fig. 35: Photo by Martha Swope pictures Balanchine, Kay Mazzo, and Martins rehearsing *Duo Concertant.*

Fig. 36: Martins dancing *Violin Concerto*.

Fig. 37: Photo by Martha Swope shows Martins, Mazzo, and Balanchine taking a bow after a performance of *Violin Concerto*.

Fig. 38: Photo by Martha Swope pictures Martins, Farrell, and Balanchine taking a bow after a performance of *Chaconne*.

Fig. 39: Photo by Martha Swope pictures Martins, Mazzo,
and Balanchine rehearsing *Violin Concerto*.

Men have more fixed and preconceived notions of themselves than women do. Men are less vulnerable and malleable than women. Balanchine felt this possibility and the flexibility of women, their generous ability to give of themselves. What he experienced in men was resistance and inflexibility. From my own youthful penchant for rebelliousness, I have been able to appreciate that female dancers will be more patient and accepting of direction than men. Working with women in dance offers more creative exploration than with men.

(Left) Fig. 40: Photo by Steven Caras pictures Martins in *Chaconne*.

A key aspect of Balanchine's genius was his profound musicality. Not all music is suitable for choreography: some music supports dance, but some is too overpowering. Balanchine knew what to pick and what not to pick. In his early dances like *Apollo,* Balanchine choreographed mostly to the melodic line. Later, he began to choreograph in counterpoint to it. His particular response to the piece itself dictates how it will be made.

Another ingenious invention of Balanchine's was to choreograph complex, iconic moments in dance, during moments in the score where others would usually not. For example, in *Serenade* there is the iconic image of the man, one woman in arabesque, and another on the floor, in which the man famously rotates the woman. The music in that moment strikes me as being not particularly moving, and yet Balanchine used it to create one of the most moving moments in dance. It's as though Tchaikovsky wanted the audience to breathe for a moment before presenting it with his next great musical theme. But Balanchine used the opportunity to allow ballet to shine, as if he concluded that he needed to help the composer transition from one theme to another.

Fig. 41: Photo by Martha Swope pictures Maria Caligari in Balanchine's *Serenade.*

Approximately fifteen seconds after that moment in *Serenade*, all three dancers walk to the upper corner of the stage and await perhaps one of the work's most famous musical passages. As only Balanchine could demonstrate, he decided not to choreograph intricate steps, or compete with the score, but instead simply had the three dancers walk diagonally across the stage. There are many similar examples in Balanchine's choreography.

Fig.42: Photo by Martha Swope pictures Geroge Balanchine, Martins, and others during a stage rehearsal at New York State Theatre.

Fig. 43: Photo by Martha Swope pictures Martins listening to music in his office, contemplating choreography.

In working with Mr. B, he said very little but let the dancer find his own way of dancing the role and his own relation to the character of the music. The music provided the key to the role, the whole character of how you were to dance to it. This was beyond the business of counting and hearing the music; it had to do with the feeling and shape and size of the sound, of matching musical scale to dance scale. I have come to think that good ballet is 90 percent music and ten percent dance.

Fig. 44: Photo by Martha Swope pictures Martins teaching NYCB in the Main Hall.

Balanchine's strength came from an ability to translate the images he saw in his mind into balletic form, and to work with dancers, not by molding them to the idea, but by knowing how these particular dancers could embody these images from their own strengths and dance personalities.

With my settling into the Company came an appreciation of Balanchine as a teacher. His class was not meant to maintain our condition but to *extend* it. Dancers and writers have often commented on Balanchine's stress on speed and clarity, but I think his key concern was *energy*. Balanchine demanded that all parts of the dancing body be energized. In class and in his ballets, Balanchine was asking for liveliness, the dancer's active presence. He asked that you show your interest, your devotion, your joy in what you were doing. And he asked that you show that dance is your life, and that your life, your act of living, is dance.

Chapter 7:

Choreographing

When I first came to the United States, I did not fully appreciate the honor of working with a living legend like Mr. B. Being ambitious myself, I wondered if I could do what he did. Another kind of schooling began, for I was not only learning roles from this master but also learning his solutions to the problems of dance.

As I wrote above, it was from Balanchine that I learned the aesthetics of good partnering. This began with his stressing of the distance the man places between himself and the woman. He always insisted we make room between ourselves. When a girl is doing unsupported work, don't just stand right behind her—get out of her way!

Fig. 45: Photo by Martha Swope pictures Peter Martins demonstrating Balanchine's technique of distance between partners to Merril Ashley and David Parsons during a rehearsal of *Barber Violin Concerto*.

No remark has been so badly misunderstood as Mr. B's, "Ballet is woman." Rather than diminishing the importance of male dancers, it was a call for men to honor women. It is a courtly and romantic notion, which requires additional responsibilities of men.

Mr. B disliked dance prima donnas. These are dancers who tend to think only of themselves and who had a hard time adjusting to the New York City Ballet's way of working. He preferred dancers who willingly and happily placed themselves at the disposal of his dance aesthetic.

In late 1976, the New York City Ballet orchestra went on strike and we could not perform at our home theatre. I gathered a small group to dance pieces from our repertory at Brooklyn College. I also asked our dancers Richard Tanner and Robert Weiss to create new pieces. Weiss picked a Fauré work. Tanner chose Schubert but also wanted to try some short orchestral pieces by Charles Ives. When Dick ran into deadline pressures, he challenged me to help him complete those. The music seemed ugly and fascinating and quirky and funny, so I agreed and began to work. I called it *Calcium Light Night*, and it proved a big success in Brooklyn.

Mr. B heard about it and, once the strike was settled, came to me and said, "I hear you did something, dear. Can I see?"

(Left) Fig. 46: Photo by Martha Swope pictures Martins rehearsing Daniel Duell and Heather Watts in *Calcium Night Light*.

We agreed to meet in a practice room at the School of American Ballet at Julliard. When Mr. B came in the dancer, Danny Duell, and I, feigned nonchalance but were in fact fighting back fits of mild terror. Balanchine sat down without a fuss and watched in complete silence. At the end he came over to me and said, "You know, wonderful."

"Really?"

"Yes, very interesting, but it's not ballet. A ballet has to have a woman. Give her some solos and then choreograph a *pas de deux.*"

I added Heather Watts, a former principal dancer at NYCB, to the ballet. He told me what he liked. It was musical, odd, and interesting. He asked if I had any costumes. I said I knew exactly what I wanted.

"Good. We'll do opening night. Okay? So long, dear."

Fourteen days later, *Calcium* premiered in New York and the press acclaimed me a choreographer. I was not convinced, but I continued to work with Heather, this time on Rossini's *Sins of My Old Age.* She suggested Sean Lavery, another former principal dancer at NYCB, as a partner, and in four days I created an extended *pas de deux.* Jerome Robbins popped his head in during rehearsal one day and asked if he could watch. After five minutes he waved and left.

That was in February, and some weeks later Mr. B told me that Jerry was planning a sketchbook for the spring season. "Jerry tells me you choreographed a pretty duet. Have you finished?"

"Yes."

Without asking to see it, he said, "Then we'll put it in."

I knew it needed some more work, however, and asked him to come see it.

"It's wonderful, you know. It's not sentimental. That's what's good about it. But maybe you should work a little bit on the ending.

"What should I do?"

Ten minutes later, he had completely rechoreographed the ending. He asked Heather and Sean to do my version, and then follow it with his. Afterwards he asked which I preferred.

"Yours."

"Why?"

"It has more surprises. It's less logical, and because of that more surprising."

"Then it's yours, for free." Then he patted my arm and off he went.

This is a complex relationship, that of master and student, and I cannot pretend it was all simple and without fear, distrust, and suspicion as well as affection, reverence, and gratitude. Yet the kind of career I have had as a dancer and choreographer would not have been possible without Balanchine's influence.

I am not psychoanalytical by nature, but I know that growing up without a father has made me overly sensitive to father figures and frantic for their approval.

Fig. 47: Photo by Martha Swope pictures Ib Andersen, Patricia McBride, and Martins rehearsing *Valse Triste*.

Fig. 48: Photo by Martha Swope pictures Martins rehearsing *Scarlatti* on stage at the New York State Theatre.

In the spring of 1979, Balanchine was recovering from an illness. I worked in collaboration with him on two projects, a section of *Tricolore* and a ballet from New York City Opera's production of *Dido and Aeneas*. As my choreographic experience was growing, I had the courage to tell Mr. B that my interest was serious. I wanted to have a project of my own, to tackle something major. I asked him if he could suggest a composer to work on. "You know something, dear? Scarlatti, interesting composer. I wanted to do something myself. I never had time." This became *Sonate di Scarlatti* (I had proposed *Giardino di Scarlatti*, but Mr. B overruled me, saying that sounded too much like a restaurant in the West Village).

Fig. 49: Photo by Martha Swope pictures Martins rehearsing
Darci Kistler and Ib Andersen in *Histoire du Soldat*.

Similarly, I thought John Adams was a great composer, but the orchestra didn't think he was a great conductor. When I became head of the Company, I asked him to consider dropping the adagio at the end of *Fearful Symmetries*, because it was so slow. John curtly said, "Then don't do it." So I rethought the entire piece and created a very surreal solution that worked well.

During the last week of August 1980, the Company was scheduled to appear at Tivoli in Copenhagen. As a tribute to Denmark, Mr. B asked me to choreograph a work to Carl Nielsen's *Lille Suite*, Opus 1. He would take the orchestral score home for a weekend, transcribe it into a piano score, and then I would choreograph the ballet from the piano score. There is no story, really, but the music suggested to me some ideas about the progress of love, and the ballet is a kind of little love story. From there we moved on to Stravinsky's *Histoire du Soldat* and, in the spring of 1981, to the Tchaikovsky festival. Later, I had the thrill of staging Drigo's *The Magic Flute*, showcasing the elegance and purity of Darci Kistler.

Fig. 50: Photo by Martha Swope pictures Martins rehearsing Darci Kistler and Ib Andersen in *Histoire du Soldat*.

Figures 51 and 52: Photos by Martha Swope picture
Kistler and Martins in *Magic Flute*.

Sleeping Beauty

One day Lincoln Kirstein burst into my office and shouted, "You're doing *Sleeping Beauty!*"

"What?"

"And you're doing it with Jerry [Robbins]."

"Lincoln, this is pure fantasy."

"Well, you're co-directors, and you have to do it."

"We can't put on *Sleeping Beauty* in the New York State Theatre," Balanchine once told me.

"Why not?" I asked.

"Because," Mr. B explained, "It doesn't have a turntable." As Mr. B explained to me, the great, old opera houses had revolving stages that allowed the audience to experience, quite literally, the changing of scenes in a single moment. I was concerned about collaborating with Robbins, although I remembered that in the *Nutcracker* Mr. B had done the ballet, Jerry did the battle scenes, and both got credit. In any case, Jerry never mentioned a possible collaboration to me, so it became clear that Lincoln had not told him about his plans.

Of course, I did not know what Balanchine's vision would have been, as he did not elaborate, but I continued with a year-long research project to examine all the other productions that had been put on worldwide. I studied the tapes of all the other productions, immersed myself in the glorious score, and recognized that Tchaikovsky often repeated phrases throughout his score. Most productions that I studied had two or, sometimes, three intermissions, but I wanted to create a streamlined version that, if possible, could function with only one intermission. That was an incredible challenge for me. I believe I found the answer, although not where one would expect an intermission to be placed. Other productions commonly placed an intermission after Aurora wakes up, following a hundred years of sleep, but I chose to take a different route, placing the intermission after the Hunt scene, just before the Prince travels to wake up Aurora.

For me, the most important thing was to highlight the great Tchaikovsky melodies in the music. In my opinion, Tchaikovsky's *Sleeping Beauty* is by far his most beautiful score, even more than *Swan Lake* and *The Nutcracker*.

Fig. 53: Photo by Paul Kolnik pictures Martins working on *Sleeping Beauty*.

After outlining the character arcs, and using the strange but useful skills in miming that I learned at the Royal Danish Ballet, I finally felt capable of producing a work that might make Balanchine proud. I remember acting out each character in the studio, to the dancers' great amusement, but it still helped them a great deal with their performances. I wanted to retain most of the great Petipa choreography and asked permission from the Balanchine Trust to incorporate Balanchine's great Garland Dance, which he had created some years earlier. They happily obliged, and this was one more ode to Balanchine, furthering his legacy in my version of *Sleeping Beauty*.

I then went to see the famous designer David Mitchell to discuss set designs, and Patricia Zipproth to discuss costumes. Mitchell built a model and spent two hours going through it with me, telling me how it would work. Zipproth had created sketches for all of the costumes even before we met, and they were brilliant. But I noted a huge problem.

"It looks very expensive. Three and a half hours. One hundred dancers. Three million dollars (in 1990). We need to raise half before I dare to announce it."

Fig. 54: Photo by Paul Kolnik pictures the *Sleeping Beauty Boat* Scene.

Fig. 55: Photo by Paul Kolnik pictures the *Sleeping Beauty* Garland Dance.

Fig. 56: Photo by Paul Kolnik pictures the *Sleeping Beauty* Hunt Scene.

Fig. 57: Photo by Paul Kolnik pictures the *Sleeping Beauty* Finale.

Fig. 58: Photo by Paul Kolnik pictures the *Sleeping Beauty* Ballroom.

We got the money and cut many of the repeats, but not any of the gorgeous music. *Sleeping Beauty* became the Company's most successful ballet other than *The Nutcracker*, and it was the biggest undertaking of my entire career. During my research, I discovered that Tchaikovsky had originally intended for the Fairy variations in Act I to run consecutively, without stops in between. However, all other productions had pauses between variations, to allow for applause. I decided to choreograph my production of *Sleeping Beauty* according to Tchaikovsky's scenario. I did, however, change some of the meters in the solos as an ode to Balanchine, who used this technique frequently, making the choreography far more interesting.

I chose to choreograph the ballet with Darci Kistler in mind. For the *pas de deux* in the last act, I chose Petipa's choreography, because there was no need to change it. His *pas de deux* was pure and elegant. It also helped that Darci danced it perfectly. The choreography fit her like a glove. However, in the last act — also known as the Jewels section — I re-choreographed Petipa's version and added a new male solo. I also added a new *pas de deux* for Red Riding Hood and the Wolf.

Fig. 59: Photo by Paul Kolnik pictures the *Sleeping Beauty*
Red Riding Hood Scene.

My favorite part was when the King and Queen abdicate in favor of
Aurora and her Prince. I was criticized by the press for that section, as
many claimed it was unrealistic for a monarchy, but Lincoln supported the
decision fully, and loved the idea. In any event, just as this book was
finalized for publication, the Queen of Denmark abdicated in favor of her
son and his princess, a commoner whom he met in a modern-day fairy tale.

Fig. 60: Photo by Paul Kolnik pictures the Epilogue of *Sleeping Beauty*.

Casting Darci Kistler in *Sleeping Beauty* was a dream come true; she was the most classically talented among the dancers, yet still poetic and youthful. Kistler came to New York from California when she was fourteen and lived in a Swiss Town House, or a dormitory, while she studied dance. One year later, Mr. B hired her. She was so advanced technically Balanchine said, "She's divine, only fifteen, and she will be the greatest ever!" I couldn't tell him I would soon be dating her.

Figures 61, 62, and 63: Photos by Paul Kolnik picture Ben Huys and Darci Kistler in the premier of *Sleeping Beauty*.

Mr. B would often say, "Don't get married." But when he was in the hospital, he asked, "What is the most important thing? Marry. Have a family." He had none, despite having been married six times. "They all left me," was all he said. I believe he was lonely. He was a father figure to Darci Kistler and me. I often wonder what would have happened to me if I hadn't met him. Half of my contemporaries are dead, either by suicide or drink.

Swan Lake

I choreographed *Swan Lake* a number of years later, for the Royal Danish Ballet in Copenhagen. I invited the great Danish painter, Per Kirkeby, to design the sets and costumes. For anyone who knows Per's work, it's no surprise that the production design was abstract, but the critics took issue with this. Nevertheless, the public loves the production, and it became an all-time best seller, following *The Nutcracker* and *Sleeping Beauty*.

Fig. 64: Photo by Paul Kolnik pictures Martins
and Per Kirkeby designing the sets for *Swan Lake*.

Fig. 65: Photo by Paul Kolnik pictures Martins
on stage with Kirkeby during a rehearsal of *Swan Lake*.

Fig. 66: Photo by Paul Kolnik pictures Martins
on stage during a rehearsal of *Swan Lake*.

Fig. 67: Photo by Paul Kolnik pictures the set of *Swan Lake* Act II.

I fundamentally re-choreographed the entirety of Act I, again choosing to honor Petipa's style. I kept, for the most part, Balanchine's version of Act II, which he had choreographed years earlier. Act III was entirely my own. I also added the national dances – Hungarian, Neapolitan, Spanish, and Russian, just to name a few.

(Left) Fig. 68: Photo by Steven Caras pictures Kistler and Corel Crabtree in Balanchine's *Swan Lake* at the School of American Ballet Workshop.

Fig. 69: Photo by Paul Kolnik pictures the Jester Dance in *Swan Lake*.

Fig. 70: Photo by Paul Kolnik pictures the Beer Dance in *Swan Lake*.

Figures 71 and 72: Photos by Paul Kolnik picture Act IV of *Swan Lake*.

Fig. 73: Photo by Paul Kolnik pictures Act IV of *Swan Lake*.

Act IV was also entirely new choreography, and has become, over the years, my favorite act. I believe Mr. B would have liked it. The ending, in my opinion, is truly powerful. When the Prince recognizes his grave mistake of choosing the Black Swan over the White Swan, he is left on stage alone and in despair. This, for me, emphasized his tragic error, and made it all the more heart-breaking to watch.

Romeo and Juliet

Some years later, I decided to mount a production of *Romeo and Juliet*. I choreographed it for Sterling Hyltin and Robby Fairchild. It was a truly stellar cast, with Darci Kistler and Jock Soto as Lord and Lady Capulet, Joaquin Deluz dancing Tybalt, and Daniel Ulbricht performing Mercutio.

This was the first full-length production where I did not pay tribute to predecessors but instead made it entirely my own. I tightened the production to include only one intermission. I flew to Denmark with Mark Stanley, NYCB's lighting designer, and Perry Silvey, our production stage manager, to meet with Per Kirkeby. What I envisioned for Per was to create a revolving set piece that could function as Juliet's bedroom, the grand ballroom in the castle, the street scenes, and the balcony scene. It was probably the most challenging week I ever spent in pre-production with a creative team. Per came up with a brilliant design and brought my vision to life. All scene changes took place in front of the audience's eyes, with no curtain or black lighting to hide them.

Fig. 74: Photo by Paul Kolnik pictures the cast of *Romeo and Juliet*, including Darci Kistler, Jock Soto, Sterling Hyltin, and Joaquin Deluz.

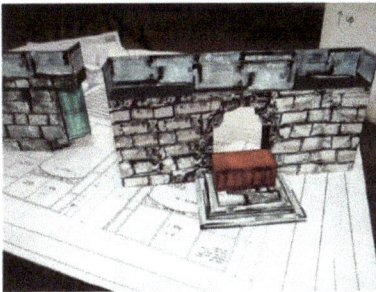

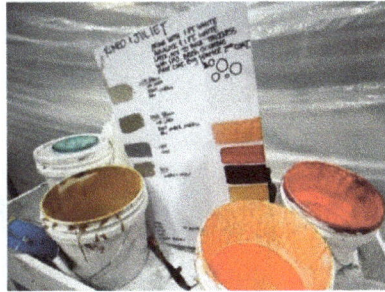

Figures 75 and 76: Photos by Paul Kolnik show the process of creating the *Romeo and Juliet* set.

Figures 77 (above) and 78 (below):
Photos by Paul Kolnik picture Kirkeby painting the set.

Fig. 79: Photo by Paul Kolnik shows Martins and Kirkeby discussing set design.

I choreographed real fighting scenes, inviting a professional stunt coordinator to train the dancers. The swords were real, which not only made the production more realistic but also testified to the commitment of the dancers at New York City Ballet. Still, it was Per's set that the audience loved most. When the ballet ends, and the set dissolves into the final tomb scene, there is always a standing ovation. And yet, Per's set was not liked by the critics. I found this utterly unfair, since he merely delivered what I had asked for, a multipurpose structure.

Fig. 80: Photo by Paul Kolnik shows Fighting Scene in *Romeo and Juliet*.

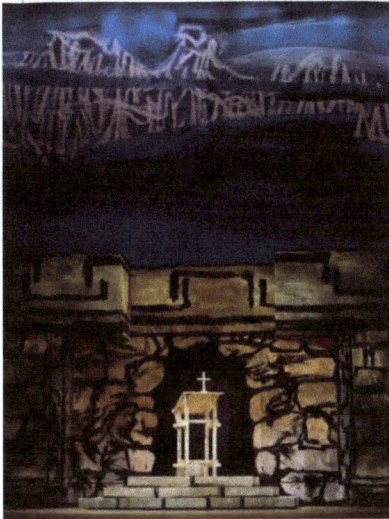

Fig. 81: Photo by Paul Kolnik shows *Romeo and Juliet* set.

Figures 82 and 83: Photos by Paul Kolnik shows Sterling Hyltin and Robert Fairchild in *Romeo and Juliet*.

Romeo and Juliet was one of my most satisfying experiences choreographing. I felt it was my most original full-length ballet, and I am proud of the production to this day.

Fig. 84: Photo by Paul Kolnik shows the line
to purchase tickets for Martins' *Romeo and Juliet*.

Ocean's Kingdom

Later in my career, in 2011, I had the great pleasure of collaborating with Paul McCartney, choreographing to his orchestral score *Ocean's Kingdom*. Paul and I discussed the ballet for it at great length in his townhouse on West 55th Street. When he came to rehearsals, he had his driver drop him off, always alone, at the stage door. He always had interesting ideas about the music and the choreography, and we enjoyed working together. But for such an amazing songwriter and musician, Paul could not read a score.

"How on earth do you compose?" I asked him when he told me that.

"It's simple," he answered. "I sit in my car and sing the melody, and when I get to my office my assistant writes it down."

We worked together for roughly a year to marry the ballet to his score. Paul recommended his daughter, Stella McCartney, to design the costumes, and I happily agreed. When the costumes were first being made, Paul quickly corrected a mistake. Some of the costumes had been made from real leather, and he was adamant that Stella would be incensed because she never allowed animal products in her designs. So we changed the costumes. Many in the audience found them, and the entire production, "visually stunning."

Fig. 85: Photo by Paul Kolnik pictures the cast of *Ocean's Kingdom*.

The ballet received mostly poor reviews, primarily from Robert Gottlieb in *The Observer* and Alastair Macaulay in the *New York Times*. I will concede that the ballet was not my best, but I still wouldn't go back and change anything. Of course, given Paul's involvement it also got tremendous publicity and sales, which was wonderful. Working with Paul was one of the most memorable experiences in my career. I grew up a huge Beatles fan, so I am still starstruck by him today. Paul and I stayed in touch for some time. He once reached me in the Salt Lake City airport at two in the morning (seven London time) and cheerily said, "Hi Peter, it's Paul!" Last year, he turned 81. Collaborating with him was always a pleasure.

• • •

I think I am at my most honest when I choreograph. I search for what is really right, what is best and clearest and most truthful. This may explain why I am so happy as a choreographer, and I owe this happiness to Mr. B. He guided me and encouraged me to be myself in my dancing and my choreography.

Figure 86: Photo by Paul Kolnik pictures Martins, Paul McCartney,
and Sara Mearns at the premier of *Ocean's Kingdom*.

Balanchine choreographed over 400 ballets, and about 75 of them are regarded as staples of his repertoire today. I have choreographed roughly 90 ballets, and I would say that out of those, about 25 are good. Ultimately, only time can judge the merit of a ballet, and which ballets last in the repertoire. Balanchine once told me that in order to make one good ballet, you have to make at least ten others, whether they be good or bad. Choreography is about practice, and the life of a choreographer is one of patience and the willingness to fail and learn from one's mistakes.

One of the great lessons my mother taught me was that we don't know what will happen in the future. Choreographing is a vulnerable process, but the greatest reward is watching the dancers bring your vision to life. Similarly, the dancing life is hard, but the greatest reward for a dancer is dancing itself. It is the most satisfying thing for a dancer to do and for a choreographer to watch. There are no fringe benefits, just the love of the craft.

Figures 87 and 88: Photos by Martha Swope picture Martins choreographing.

Chapter 8:

Succession

George Balanchine taught me everything—music, literature, decency, art, the visual arts, integrity, and good taste.

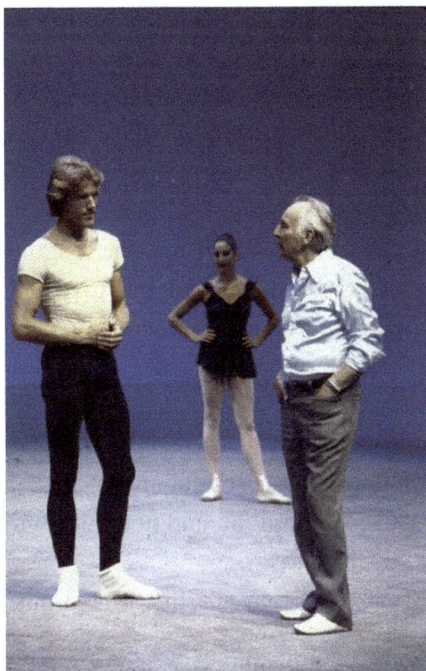

Fig. 89: Photo by Martha Swope pictures Martins and Balanchine during the filming of *Violin Concerto*.

Proportion is all. There was an absolutely beautiful girl in the Company of Russian descent. She was exquisite and perfectly proportioned. One couldn't take one's eyes off of her. However, Balanchine was frustrated by her lack of technique and inability to learn. One day in Company class, he compared her to a male dancer who, although incredibly technically talented and bright, had unfortunate proportions. Mr. B said, "if only you could have his mind, and if only you could have her proportions, there would be a God." He said this in front of all the dancers in class who, reasonably, were shocked. I was fortunate enough that Balanchine thought I possessed both somewhat good proportions and a good mind.

Walking home one night Mr. B exclaimed, "There's no such thing as a perfect body ... it doesn't exist. It's like a perfect marriage where people can listen to and learn from each other. How often do you see that?"

"You know what's wrong with you? Your knees are one inch too low!"

I went home and looked at myself in the mirror, stark naked. He was absolutely right!

But Mr. B was always unbelievably supportive. "Don't be so stubborn, young Danish boy who knows nothing," he would say in his avuncular way. "I'm a very good cook. I take care of my plants. And you know what you are? You ... are a blade of grass."

One day I got a call from Rudolf Bing, the longtime general manager of the Metropolitan Opera, who asked me to dance *Giselle* with the National Ballet Company of Canada on a Monday night in the opera house the following week. He offered me $10,000, which was a lot of money at the time. "I don't know *Giselle*," I answered, and Bing said, "We will send someone to teach it to you." It was a great opportunity, but when I asked Mr. B for permission he said, "Absolutely not. You belong to us."

"But Mr. B, it's a Monday night, and nothing is going on."

"No."

"But Mr. B, I want to buy an apartment, and this will help with the down payment."

"You don't need a big apartment. A studio is enough."

At the time, Peter Schaufuss, a fellow Dane, was living with me, and I recommended him to Mr. B, who auditioned him and liked him. Then Peter (known as "Little Peter" and I was called "Big Peter") got a call from Rudolf Bing offering *Giselle* and accepted. When he told me this I said, "Let me give you some advice. You have to ask Mr. B for permission." Little Peter was defiant and refused to do so.

Rudolf Bing then called Mr. B and said, "George, I don't understand. Big Peter can't do *Giselle*, but Little Peter can?"

"I never gave Little Peter permission."

The next day, Barbara Horgan, Mr. B's assistant, told me a telegram had been sent to Little Peter that read, "Your services are no longer required." *Finito*! For years afterward Little Peter thought I had been involved and our friendship was never the same, but I wasn't. Mr. B was like that, very decisive when he felt his authority was being disrespected.

The next time I met with Mr. B, he reached for his personal checkbook and wrote me a check for $10,000. I took that check, held it up and tore it into shreds.

Mr. B was shocked and said, "Why are you doing that?"

"Because you can't bribe me."

Mr. B turned white and left in a huff, but in retrospect I believe that was when he began to consider me as a worthy successor, because I had demonstrated integrity.

I spent over a decade as principal dancer, and then Mikhail Baryshnikov defected from the Soviet Union's Kirov Ballet, as it was known then (today it is again the Mariinsky), and subsequently joined the Company. Although he wasn't tall, he had a perfectly proportioned body and I thought the world of his dancing, which was even somewhat intimidating. I was 6'1" and could dance with anyone. Misha was only 5'7," but could only dance with the short girls. I had very long arms and could bring girls back if they fell to one side. Nevertheless, he was truly the best at everything. Despite some insecurity on my part, we became great friends.

During our summer season at the Saratoga Performing Arts Center, Misha and I shared a home. One day the phone rang at 7am, and Mr. B was on the line.

"Meet me at Sperry's at 7:30." I was surprised it was me he was calling to meet, and not Misha.

When I got to the restaurant, he sipped his coffee and pointed to himself. "You want this job?" I was 31 and didn't know what to say.

"You're always around, and you don't miss anything."

"Well, maybe."

"Do you know what it entails?"

"No."

"You have to do EVERYTHING! The costume shop. Take care of the Russian seamstresses. The production staff. Those stagehands know everything! The ushers. Be kind to them. The enormous orchestra – 70 players. Make sure they're happy! Management. Marketing. You have to choose all the photos and images. And most important, the School of American Ballet. Only hire American dancers. You need a unified style. Fundraising. *You* have to do it. You don't have Lincoln, like I did. You have to nourish the entire organization. You have to inspire everyone. You have to nurture. You have to lead with kindness!

Figures 90 and 91: Photos by Martha Swope picture Martins (left) and Martins with Debbie Koolish (right) in his office, shortly after he accepted the role of 'Joint Ballet Master in Chief'.

When the Board of Directors, specifically Gillian Attfield, approached me about taking over the position, I carefully considered the responsibilities that it required, and was, in some ways, nervous to accept it. I asked if Jerry Robbins had been contacted with the same proposal, and they said yes and that he agreed to share the responsibility with me, providing that he did not sit in the back seat, but in the passenger seat.

Subsequently, I met with Jerry to discuss our partnership, and he proposed that we both receive the title of Ballet Master in Chief. I told Jerry that historically there is only one chief, and he replied that I must accept it, despite my fears that it could be confusing to the public to have two chiefs. Nevertheless, I accepted it. I told Gillian Attfield that my primary reason for accepting the task at hand was that I had witnessed Balanchine's struggle to create a place for ballet in America and so I felt it especially important that his efforts were not in vain. It was Balanchine's legacy that I wanted to uphold, and so that is what I did. I felt, and still feel to this day, that preserving and expanding his wishes are my greatest accomplishments.

Fig. 92: Photo by Martha Swope shows Peter Martins and
Jerry Robbins as co-directors in 1983, the year Mr. Balanchine passed.

•   •   •

One day Balanchine was standing in the wings watching a live performance. He asked me, "Which is more important, the New York City Ballet, or the School of American Ballet? I hesitated and said, "The Ballet." He shook his head, and I knew I had made a mistake. "The School?" He shook his head again. "No, both. They are *interdependent.* Both are equally important!"

Fig. 93: Photo by Paul Kolnik pictures Peter Martins
in the wings at David Koch Theatre.

It is imperative, in my opinion, that one individual run both the School
of American Ballet and the New York City Ballet. It was Lincoln Kirstein
who appointed me Chairman of the Faculty at SAB. There was a culture
instilled by Balanchine that protected faculty: Balanchine never fired
teachers due to old age, and I honored that tradition myself.

Among the first initiatives I instituted at the school was creating a
senior class for both boys and girls on Saturdays, emphasizing partnering.
It was truly the first partnering class of substance that SAB ever had. Not
only was it very productive and instructive, but the students and I had so
much fun. I would take excerpts from various ballets – challenging ballets
– and prepare the students for what a career at NYCB would really entail,
because it is a Company where partnering is paramount.

One of the most popular teachers at SAB was Darci Kistler. I
sometimes would watch the end of her classes and marvel at 30 or so girls
and boys embracing her. Of course, it ended up looking more like a dog
pile, because not all of them could reach her. Darci has a beautiful spirit
and it showed in her teaching. The last five or ten minutes of her children's
class, she would ask the students what they wanted to do and just let them

dance. Sometimes she would put a piece of clothing in the center of the room and the kids would do the jump of their choice diagonally across the room. She let them have so much fun, which has always inspired me.

The process of selection of apprentices into the NYCB was based entirely on merit. Obviously, we had a limited budget regarding how many new dancers could be hired each year. Annually, I would accept on average five to eight students to join the Company as apprentices. Apprentices are essentially understudies for the corps de ballet. They learn the repertoire, and often participate in performances when a large cast is needed. Each apprenticeship lasts between one and two years, after which time most are accepted into the Company, although not all. As for those students who are not accepted as apprentices into the New York City Ballet, they often go on to have great careers at other prestigious ballet companies.

For Mr. B, the Company and the school were equally important because, as he put it, "the Company shows the students at SAB how to dance, and SAB provides the Company with the continued lineage of its desired aesthetic."

In 2009, the School of American Ballet was awarded the National Medal of Arts. I was invited to the White House to accept the award and found myself standing on a small stage with President Barack Obama. Realizing that it would be a couple of minutes before the ceremony commenced, I tried my best to engage in conversation, however awkwardly. I started out, quite boldly, asking if what I had heard – that his daughters were interested in ballet and had begun taking classes – was true. All he said was, "You bet." I was unsure how to respond and so for a moment I was silent. I decided to inquire further and told the President that I might, if he wished, be able to teach his daughters a thing or two about ballet. Again, he simply replied, "I bet." My conversation with the President of the United States consisted of three words from him.

. . .

I came to learn that not only were the school and the Company equally important, but that the orchestra was, too. One of the biggest dilemmas we faced one year was the orchestra going on strike during the Christmas season *Nutcracker* run, which produced a major portion of our annual revenue. I still wonder what Mr. B would have done. He was so pure. But when I learned that technology existed to go to tape without in any way sacrificing artistic quality, I decided to confront the union. What management wanted was a rational work rule: if you played a rehearsal, you had to play the performance too. After an extended struggle, we broke them. Yes, there were threats against me and my family, and some musicians never spoke to me again, but others said the union leadership had been selfish and wrong and that I had done the right thing.

· · ·

New York City Ballet faced another challenge while I was running it. In 2001, the New York City Ballet was on a European tour. We found ourselves in Parma, Italy, on September 11. I happened to be suffering from food poisoning at the time and being mostly confined to my hotel room, where I was watching the news. It was then that I witnessed the twin towers imploding.

I was petrified and grief stricken. It was the most horrific act of terror I had seen in my lifetime. I thus called the Company together for an emergency meeting. Many of the dancers were sobbing, as they had friends and family who worked in the towers. I asked how they wanted to proceed: either to perform our premiere in Parma, or not. When they begged me not to make them perform, I canceled our premiere. The unknown for so many of them was crippling, and I thought it would be cruel, to say the least, to require them to dance.

The director of the theater and the mayor of Parma were understanding. They accompanied me in front of the curtain to address the audience, who had already been seated in the theater. The audience was also understanding and gave us all a standing ovation. I was incredibly moved by their empathy and compassion. We were entering into what I knew was a global crisis, and the support we received gave me hope that we were not alone.

· · ·

With respect to my relationship with each dancer, I remember vividly a conversation with Misha – who at the time was running American Ballet Theatre – and was adamant that any dancer who came to his office only received ten minutes maximum. I, on the other hand, felt very differently. I thought that putting a time limit on any of my dancers' visits was wrong. Sometimes they would stay only five minutes, and other times they would stay an hour or more. Either way, I felt it was my duty to support them. The issues were not always dance related. There were times when I felt I was not a ballet director, but a therapist. I did my best to ease their pain, and I can only hope that I succeeded in some way. I always wanted every dancer to walk out of my office smiling, not crying.

. . .

Figures 94, 95, and 96: Photos by Martha Swope show Balanchine and Martins rehearsing *Union Jack, Vienna Waltzes, and Tzigane.*

. . .

Programming was an entirely different beast. I once went to Mr. B and asked why we weren't doing *Agon*, because we hadn't done it for four or five years. His response was, "No dear, you have to take it away for a while so people don't stop appreciating it.

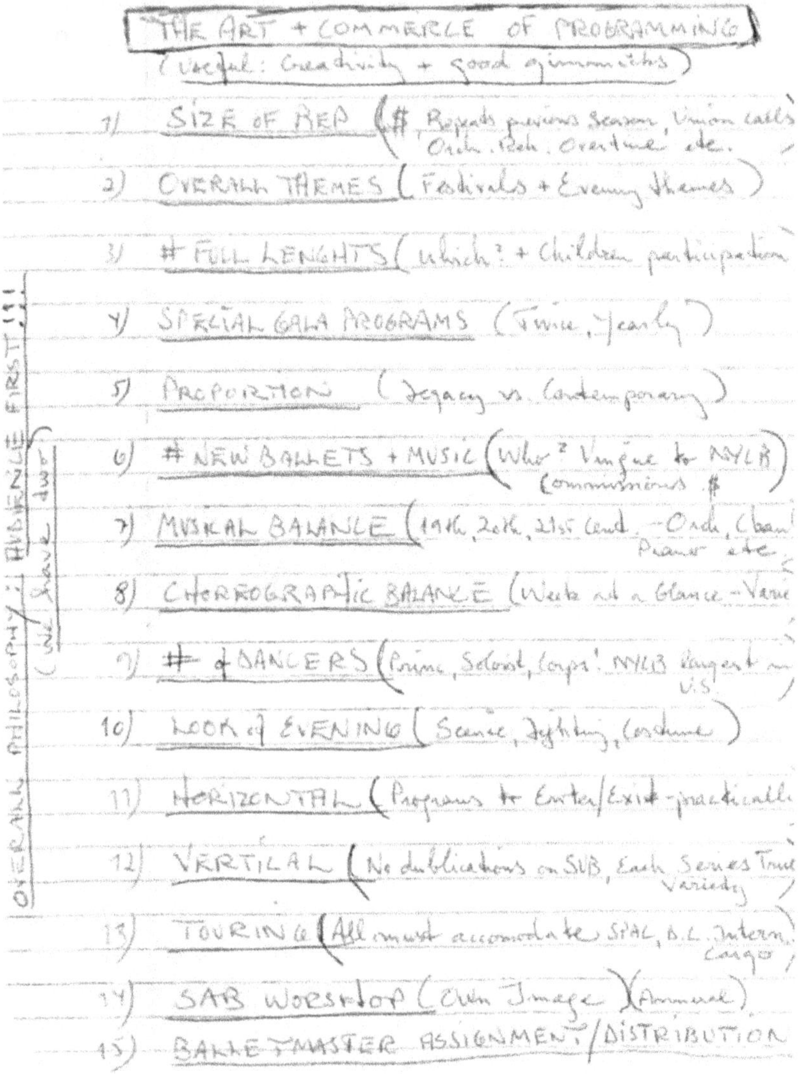
THE ART + COMMERCE OF PROGRAMMING

1) SIZE OF REP
2) OVERALL THEMES (Festivals + Evening themes)
3) # FULL LENGHTS (which? + Children participation
4) SPECIAL GALA PROGRAMS (Twice, Yearly)
5) PROPORTION (Legacy vs. Contemporary)
6) # NEW BALLETS + MUSIC
7) MUSICAL BALANCE
8) CHOREOGRAPHIC BALANCE
9) # of DANCERS
10) LOOK of EVENING (Scenic, lighting, costume)
11) HORIZONTAL
12) VERTICAL
13) TOURING
14) SAB WORKSHOP
15) BALLETMASTER ASSIGNMENT/DISTRIBUTION

OVERALL PHILOSOPHY :: AUDIENCE FIRST !!!

Fig. 97: Photo of a list Martins wrote outlining the "Art and Commerce of Programming".

When I became sole Ballet Master in Chief, I took Balanchine's entire body of work and divided it into three sections. The first included his masterpieces, the second his great ballets, and the last his good ballets, which are still better than anyone else's to date. Some of those I considered to be his masterpieces were *Agon, Liebeslieder, Divertimento No. 15, Apollo, Concerto Barocco, Serenade, Symphony in C, Piano Concerto No. 2, Union Jack,* and *Theme and Variations.* His great ballets include *Symphony in Three Movements, Scotch Symphony, Tchaikovsky Pas de Deux, Tarantella, Valse Fantasy,* and *Vienna Waltzes.* Some of his good ballets were *Donizetti Variations, Tzigane, Firebird,* and *Kammermusik.* As anyone can see, he had more good ballets than great ballets, and more great ballets than masterpieces.

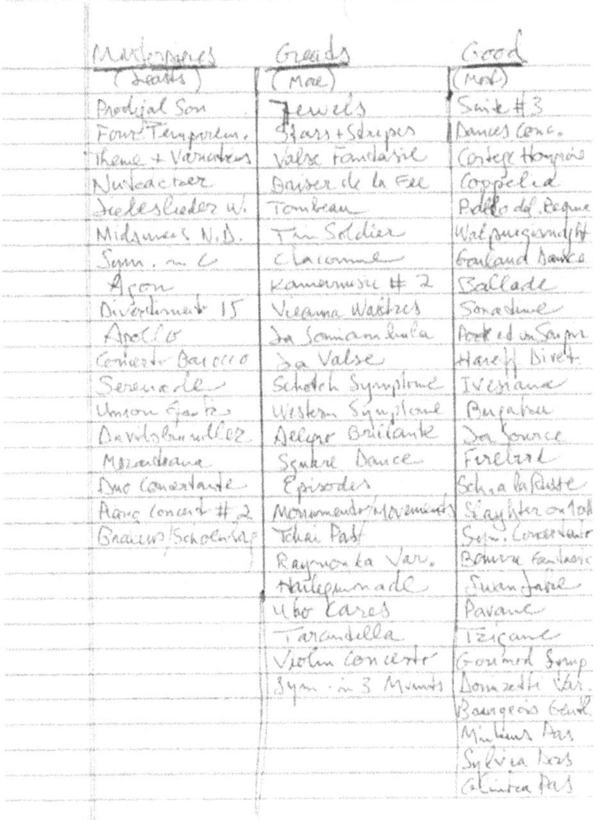

Fig. 98: Martins' list of Balanchine ballets,
rated on a scale from "Masterpiece" to "Good".

Mr. B would entirely disapprove of this categorization, as he often said there is no such thing as a masterpiece. Yet I believe he truly did create them. So, when it came to programming, I always kept his words in the back of my mind. I created programming that was diverse so that no one would lose appreciation for any of his works.

•   •   •

Fundraising was a professional challenge for me, insofar as I never considered myself a professional in that capacity, though many of my friends on the Board suggested that I could be enormously helpful. I must say I had a special affinity for elder ladies with a big capacity to donate. There was one woman whom I visited every Sunday morning at her apartment on the Upper East Side but was no longer capable of attending performances due to her age. I would bring her videotapes of ballets and we would sit, smoke together, and watch them. She was ecstatic and loved the moments and ended up being one of our largest donors, even upon her death.

Another donor, Irene Diamond, who became a close friend, was enormously generous. I would also visit her in her apartment and talk about my vision for the future of New York City Ballet. In addition, I invited any member of the Board and contributors who were interested to my office between 6:30 and 7:30pm to hear me tell stories about Balanchine, in particular, but Lincoln Kirstein as well. The close relationship I had with donors is what increased the endowment threefold. Donors were most inclined to give because of the stories I shared about Balanchine. I suppose that was my way of fundraising, even though I had no previous knowledge of how to do it. It surely, in the end, did contribute to the bottom line. It was not only my efforts with donors, but my commitment to festivals, or "gimmicks," as Mr. B called them, that helped raise money.

Fig. 99: Photo by Martha Swope pictures
Martins with Ray Charles during the production of *Fool for You*.

• • •

Before offering me the position, Mr. B insisted I have a "gimmick." He said to me one day, "I came up with Stravinsky for the festival of 1972. What's yours?"

I conceived an American music festival with promotional posters by Andy Warhol, Helen Frankenthaler, Keith Haring, and Roy Lichtenstein. The music was by Charles Ives, among others. I also staged marketable programs. I put on Russian programs, including music solely by Glinka, whom Balanchine proclaimed the "father of Russian music." In addition, I devised programs that emphasized French composers such as Debussy, Ravel, and Bizet. I also made sure that German composers were represented in our programs. Bach, Mozart, and Brahms were all included and received their own special evenings.

I took the idea of "gimmick" to new heights, however. Having always had a keen interest in architecture, I wanted to create a marriage between architecture and choreography, and thus I initiated the Calatrava Project. I sought out candidates and thought Santiago Calatrava the best. I was surprised at his willingness to collaborate and elated that I was eventually able to win him over. We worked together for two years, until the Spring Gala in 2010, when our collaboration was finally brought to life.

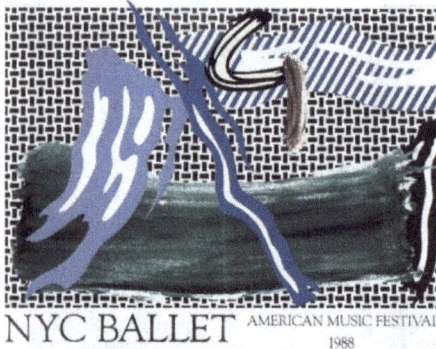

(Left) Fig. 100: Lichtenstein American Music Festival Promotional Poster.

One day I had bought a very expensive Spanish wine to impress him, and he poured some of it in my ashtray and made numerous drawings of his ideas with the wine itself. He then dipped his index finger in the wine and painted his vision.

Calatrava and I developed a great relationship, and he was engaged one hundred percent throughout the project. He designed numerous architectural structures for many of the choreographers I had invited to NYCB, including Alexey Ratmansky, Christopher Wheeldon, and Benjamin Millepied, and myself. Many, if not all were spectacular. I hoped that we could hang the displays from the ceiling in the lobby, but that proved impossible. Yet we were still able to have some of his designs displayed on the promenade. Famous for, among other things, the Oculus World Trade Center Transportation Hub in lower Manhattan. Calatrava proved to be an enormous inspiration for me, with his knowledge and appreciation of my own art form. I am, to this day, incredibly grateful to him for his tremendous contribution to the New York City Ballet. I am equally grateful to Esa-Pekka Salonen. Esa was commissioned to write a violin concerto for my ballet, which he did and came to conduct. That was the greatest musical contribution to the festival as a whole.

· · ·

In the months before Balanchine died, I was running the Company and would visit him in the hospital to keep him informed of our activities. I would ask him to do the casting of upcoming ballets. He said, "It's up to you. I'm of no use. But make *evolutionary* changes, not revolutionary ones." It was terribly painful to watch him slip away.

Mr. B died of Creutzfeldt-Jakob Disease in April 1983. He was 79. He began to lose his balance first and then became progressively weaker. On the day he died the New York City Ballet performed as per our schedule. He would have wanted it that way.

When Mr. B summoned me to Sperry's – for perhaps the most important breakfast of my life – our operating budget was $16 million, and the endowment just $6 million. After my 35 year tenure, the operating budget was $70 million, and the endowment had risen to over $200 million.

Chapter 9:

The New York Choreographic Institute

In 1998, I started The Choreographic Workshop for young choreographers from around the world to give them a chance to create new works. If it worked, we would have also developed a new generation of choreographers. They were young, inexperienced. and not well known. Irene Diamond believed in young choreographers and supported the idea, so I decided to call it The Diamond Project. Our development office disliked that idea because they thought it might preclude us from getting funds from Philip Morris, among other major corporate sponsors and foundations. But I insisted.

Other generous donors, including Daniel Shapiro and Agnes Gund, came aboard as well, and we were off to the races. As in any endeavor, there were different opinions about what we should be doing. My original purpose was to provide free rehearsal time for young choreographers. Others, like Daniel, had more expansive ideas and wanted to create an archive, or perhaps even a museum of choreography. But there was enormous good will and we worked through these issues in a civilized and constructive way.

One Sunday morning, I went to Irene's apartment and told her, "Great artists usually work by themselves—writers, composers, painters. They work alone – beginning, building, refining or sometimes throwing out altogether and starting afresh.

"But choreographers do not have that luxury. They need dancers, pianists and studios, which all cost a lot of money."

Mr. B worked on the principle of a ballet taking two hours to choreograph for every minute. He once said, "I take one hour for every minute, but I'm the fastest. Jerry takes six hours to the minute."

I wanted to create something that didn't yet exist. I told Irene, "I want to bring in the best young talent for two weeks and let them work on a piece. In the end, if they're happy, we won't have a performance but a showing, for family and friends."

People would submit their audition tapes to my associates and me, and after reviewing them we would select the most promising. Our first two choreographers at the Institute in 2000 were Alexey Ratmansky and Christopher Wheeldon. Today they are recognized as the two leading choreographers in the world.

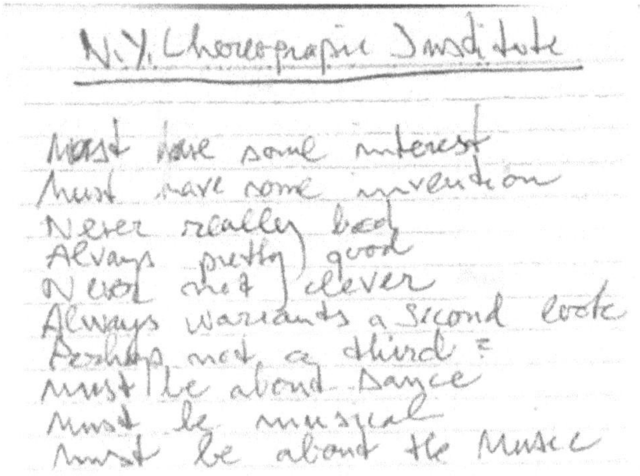
N.Y. Choreographic Institute

Must have some interest
Must have some invention
Never really bad
Always pretty good
Not that clever
Always warrants a second look
Perhaps not a third
Must be about Dance
Must be musical
Must be about the Music

Fig. 101: Martins' list of notes and requirements for prospective Choreographic Institute candidates.

From the start, I said there was no requirement to present the Institute's work in public. It was more of a workshop for developing new work. But when a young Christopher Wheeldon came to me and said he didn't think the *pas de deux* he had choreographed was up to being presented publicly, I tried to persuade him otherwise. "It's a process," I told him, and he eventually acquiesced. That piece ended up becoming the main *pas de deux* in his celebrated ballet *Polyphonia*.

As time went on, we added new initiatives. When Denise Saul joined the Board, her first contributions were running the Guild luncheon and supporting children's programs. But she began attending rehearsals, got to know many of the dancers, and helped me start the New Combinations Fund, which financed many new works.

Irene Diamond generously gave $5 million to endow the Institute and a further $500,000 to cover operating expenses for the first year. Our endowment is now over $20 million. She wanted to call it the Peter Martins Institute, but I declined and it retained the name New York Choreographic Institute. Over 100 choreographers have gone through the program. In 2020, it celebrated its 20th anniversary and everyone considers it a great success. I am extremely proud of what it has achieved in the world of ballet.

Chapter 10:

Anecdotes and Accolades

Anecdotes

When Mr. B offered me a contract for $400 a week to come to New York. I asked for $500 and got it. After six months he offered me a full contract.

After our initial awkwardness, he put me in everything. I was immediately established as a principal dancer and was featured in the *New Yorker's* "Talk of the Town" column. Violette Verdy had told Mr. B I was too cold, and Mr. B replied, "Yes, like a diamond."

We did *Coppelia*, and I asked to be in it. "You are too big," Mr. B told me. I did the part of Franz anyway, and he said, "You were fantastic! You knew you could do it, even though I didn't know you could do it."

(Left) Fig. 102: Photo by Martha Swope pictures Martins in *Coppelia* when he first arrived in New York.

• • •

Jerome Robbins was a genius at some things but very difficult to work with. He idolized Balanchine but was paranoid about me. He thought I would try to drive him out. The reverse was true, and I tried very hard to keep him happy. When I got to know Leonard Bernstein, he told me, "Jerry fucked up some of my best music." He was referring to *Age of Anxiety,* among others.

Fig. 103: Photo by Steven Caras shows Martins in *Coppelia*.

• • •

When I was a teenager, my biggest ambition was to become a conductor. I would go into my little room at home, put Tchaikovsky on the stereo and conduct to it. Conducting was always a passion of mine. When I got to the New York City Ballet, I would do it in rehearsals, sometimes to the annoyance of our own conductors. "That's our job," they would protest, but I couldn't help myself. I have always had very strong opinions about tempi and would let them know when I thought the music was too fast or too slow.

In any event, I was fascinated by Leonard Bernstein and often went to the New York Philharmonic to watch him conduct. In due course, we became friends and would talk in his dressing room. It was there that he made disparaging remarks about how Jerry Robbins had underserved his music. He continued to invite me, and when he died, in 1990, I was surprised and very touched that his office sent me a beautiful little antique silver ashtray, as a memento of our friendship. In 2004, I was able to choreograph a ballet to one of my favorites among his compositions, *The Chichester Psalms,* as a tribute to him.

• • •

I wanted to come to America because of *West Side Story*, which Jerome Robbins had choreographed on Broadway in 1957. On numerous occasions, long before we were co-directors, I urged Jerry to consider mounting a New York City Ballet production. He always rejected the suggestion, but I was persistent. Even after Jerry withdrew from his co-directorship of NYCB, perhaps because he was suspicious of my intentions, he finally agreed to mount a condensed production of *West Side Story* (*West Side Story Suite*) for the New York City Ballet. This was utterly gratifying, as my initial desire to come to America had been because of Jerry's original production. This indicated to me that Jerry finally understood that my intentions were positive and helped elevate our relationship to one of trust.

. . .

Perhaps because I'm an immigrant, I had a particular appreciation for what I think are two purely American innovations — Jazz and Modern Dance. Luckily, jazz was fortunate enough to recruit Winton Marsalis as its leader. Beginning in 1987, he brought the art form to Lincoln Center, where in 1996 it became a fully constituent department. Similarly, I had always dreamt of an American modern dance company that would be able to incorporate all its various iterations into a unified entity, as was done at New York City Ballet. I envisioned programs consisting of works by Martha Graham, Merce Cunningham, and Paul Taylor. Another night, there would be Mark Morris, Twyla Tharp, Lar Lubovich, and José Limón.

I think it's a shame that such a company does not exist. Modern dance, in my opinion, is not represented in its totality at Lincoln Center, which I always felt was a loss for the art form. I once met with Merce and his leadership board in my office to propose this idea. The problem, I suggested, is that every modern dance company is named after its choreographer and founder, resulting in the exclusion of other choreographic works. Merce was not enthralled with the idea of dropping his name from the company's title, but Paul Taylor once said he was open to this idea. I suggested that he do what Balanchine did: retitle the company and bill it as "Founded by Paul Taylor." Creating a company called "American Modern Dance" would honor all the great American innovators. My dream was ultimately to have it become another constituent department of Lincoln Center with annual seasons. Unfortunately, Paul passed away, and the idea has still not come to fruition.

Fig. 104: Photo by Steven Caras shows Martins in *Orpheus*.

• • •

The famous Noguchi lyre from *Orpheus*, an iconic image of New York City Ballet, now sits above the box office in the David Koch Theater. I had the image enlarged and hung there because it was important to me to relay to visiting companies that this was still the home of New York City Ballet.

• • •

I used to have differences with Jerry Robbins when we were co-directors. He always wanted to promote the beautiful girls, even if they couldn't dance. "Come on, Jerry," I would say, "dancers are intelligent, they know when they can't dance, you're doing them a disservice to advance them when they don't deserve it."

On the other hand, there was an extremely talented, highly intelligent, and technically perfect dancer named Gen Horiuchi that I fought to promote over Jerry's opposition, because Jerry thought he was too short, or so he said. I finally got my way, and today Gen is the longtime director of the Saint Louis Ballet. The same thing happened with another imperfect body but uncanny dancer, Daniel Duell, whom Balanchine promoted nonetheless, and who went on to become the leader of Ballet Chicago.

Fig. 105: Photo by Steven Caras shows Martins and Jerome Robbins in the Main Hall at New York State Theatre.

· · ·

Lincoln Kirstein approached Balanchine to take over the Ballet Society in 1932, when the Paris Opera declined to give him the directorship. At that time, ballet was non-existent in America. Balanchine had to build an audience for it. He opened the New York City Ballet at the City Center in 1948, to half-empty houses at best, but he created a series of masterpieces: *Orpheus, Symphony in C,* and many others.

Despite Lincoln Kirstein having recruited Balanchine to come to New York, and the fact that they had to appear together at curtain calls, Mr. B and Kirstein had no personal relationship. They were very different people. Kirstein, unlike Mr. B, frequently lost his temper badly and used gutter language.

One day Lincoln barged into the elevator at Juilliard as I was going up to the noon class. He was sweaty, pasty-faced, and trembling.

"My goodness, Lincoln, whatever is wrong?"

"You won't believe what that son of a bitch just said to me."

"What?"

"He said, 'Lincoln, the solution to your problem is simple. Just buy a gun and shoot yourself!'"

. . .

In fairness to Mr. B, Kirstein was impossible to get along with. He came to my office one night and gave me a letter addressed to the editorial board of the *New York Times* that demeaned Jerome Robbins, whom he hated and wanted fired. At the bottom were our two names, and Lincoln had already affixed his signature next to his. "Lincoln, this is nuts," I said. "It will cause a huge scandal and be all over the media. I won't do it." But Lincoln was adamant about getting rid of him and went on and on about why he was such a detriment to the New York City Ballet.

I finally said to Lincoln Kirstein, "I'm so grateful to you and Mr. B."

"Why?"

"Because Mr. B taught me everything to do, and you taught me everything NOT to do."

"Fuck you," was all he said.

Another time, Lincoln called me in and told me that the time had come to oust Mr. B himself. "He's old and getting sicker. We have to move on.

I have a plan." Obviously, it was a plan I wanted no part of, and, in the end, of course, it came to nothing.

. . .

Mr. B could be tricky, though. One day, he said he wanted me to do a ballet to Schubert, and I threw myself into researching the composer's music, which I came to love. I choreographed *Schubertiade* with three principal couples and a large corps de ballet. When I had finished, I showed it to Mr. B. After only three notes he said, "What is this? I said Schumann, not Schubert!" I was stunned, but he put *Schubertiade* on the stage anyway.

Fig. 106: Photo by Paul Kolnik shows Martins, Watts, and Farrell being directed by George Balanchine during a rehearsal of *Davidsbündlertänze*.

Fig.107: Photo by Martha Swope pictures Balanchine bowing
following the performance of one of his last ballets, *Davidsbündlertänze*.

He also did *Davidsbündlertänze*, to Schumann. It was the last ballet he choreographed, along with *Mozartiana*, which he produced simultaneously. He wasn't well. One day we waited for him for two hours in the studio. Finally, he arrived looking pale and asked me to do the beer dance for four boys and then bring in the four girls. "I can't, Mr. B, it has to be you." He looked at me, irritated, and then left the room. But then he returned in his dance shoes and choreographed it in 90 minutes. It was incredible.

. . .

When Rudolf Nureyev came to him and wanted to stage *Apollo,* Mr. B said, "OK, but you have to give me $50,000." And Balanchine gave that money to the School of American Ballet.

Rudy was extremely intelligent and well read, but he came on to everyone, which sometimes was off-putting. He called me "The Danish Princess." Once in the late 1970s, he asked me to marry him, long before that was either legal or accepted. I said, "I'm sorry, Rudy, but I'm not like you. I like girls, not boys."

"You don't know what you're missing!" he would say.

Mr. B said of him, "He's famous, he's rich, but he's not a very good dancer." He said to Rudy, "When you stop acting like a princess, I'll invite you to dance."

Rudy, who unfortunately died of AIDS at only 55, always wore a wool cap in his last years because he lost his hair and needed to keep warm. Rudy was always an inspiration to me, and his loss affected me deeply.

. . .

Another time we were doing *Orpheus*, a ballet I knew intimately, having danced the title role for years. One day Mr. B came in and said, "Not enough people on the stage. Double it to sixteen from eight." I did something I thought was ingenious. I used the same material for a larger group. I did not actually invent new steps but expanded the choreography. When it was done and Mr. B could see it would work very well, I asked him, "How do you want to handle the playbill?"

"What do you mean?"

"Do you want it to say 'additional choreography by Peter Martins?'"

"Absolutely not. You did not choreograph anything. You just expanded it."

Another time Mr. B decided I should choreograph to music by Domenico Scarlatti. I studied Scarlatti hard and choreographed a ballet of 25 minutes for four couples. Mr. B said it was a masterpiece, but added, "the public won't know that for at least ten years."

Fig. 108: Photo by Steven Caras pictures Martins rehearsing *Scarlatti*.

. . .

Mr. B was extremely diligent. He worked sixteen hours a day, seven days a week. Jerry worked two to three hours a day and was bored by many administrative details, so he didn't attend to them. As such, the Board was in awe of Balanchine. He only went to the Board twice: once to ask for earthquake relief funds in Italy, and the other to buy bullet proof vests for the NYPD. The Board trusted him. It was impossible to succeed him, but I wanted to protect him. He never spoke badly about others and was the true founder of ballet in America.

Balanchine's balletic masterpieces included *Serenade*, his first ballet in America, among many others. Mr. B absolutely hated Shostakovich and would not program him, but he loved Stravinsky and Tchaikovsky. Nevertheless, he once told me not to program *Serenade* if, as he said, "the public doesn't want to see it." He gave all those ballets to companies in Boston, Pittsburgh, Chicago, and San Francisco to help grow the art form and its audience.

• • •

Jacques d'Amboise was a great dancer, but Mr. B called him a "frail elephant" because he was so often injured. Once we were performing *Brahms/Schoenberg*, which ran for 40 minutes in four movements. It was a beautiful piece but underappreciated. I always danced the first movement and understudied the finale. One night after dancing the first movement, Mr. B knocked on the door and came in. "You have to dance the fourth movement tonight. Jacques can't go on."

"You can't be serious."

"You have plenty of time. It's only the second movement."

The dresser came in. The costume didn't fit. The sleeves were too short. Mr. B took me through the steps, and I tried to remember everything. Suzanne Farrell danced her solo movement, went on pointe, and then extended her hand to me. Exhausted from my own first movement solo, I rushed out from the wings to take her hand, and she said, "It's about time."

It went well, and afterwards there was wild applause. Mr. B said, "Dear, I knew you could do it."

Jacques d'Amboise never spoke to me. He knew then that I was slated to replace him. The lesson I took was always to be on guard. On standby.

Some years later there was another knock on the door. Helgi Tómasson was injured, and I had to dance the Donizetti *Variations,* which I didn't know, because Misha, who was the understudy, had gone missing. We were supposed to have dinner together at a Russian restaurant on the East Side, and he had slipped out before me.

"You can't be serious."

Mr. B said, "I'll teach you. In one hour." He began singing the score, took his jacket off and taught me every step. Kay Mazzo came in at 7:45 and took me through the *pas de deux.* Then the dresser came with the costume.

Finally, I said, "I have one stipulation."

"Oh. Really?"

"At least give me one more performance." (He never did.)

I made one mistake in the last movement, but otherwise it went well. Again, there was tremendous applause. "You see, dear, you *could* do it. Nice job."

It was the same with *Apollo.* Mr. B took the birth scene out when Misha joined the Company. Then one day Mr. B cast me. I had danced it many times before with the birth scene in.

"What do I do?"

"You'll figure it out."

So I made my own version. It was very abstract, but it worked. Balanchine trusted me.

He did this to other dancers, too. Once he cast Darci on a Thursday for her to dance the following Tuesday. He liked to make his dancers sink or swim. Clive Barnes once asked, "Why doesn't he prepare his people?"

Fig. 109 (top) and 110 (bottom): Photos by Steven Caras picture Martins in *Apollo*.

. . .

One day during the Ravel Festival, in 1976, Balanchine came in and said, "I have great idea – *Schéhérazade*. You want to be in it?"

"I would love it."

Next day the schedule went up, and it was given to Edward Villella.

"Mr. B, what happened?"

"I have to take care of *everyone*."

To make up for it he put me into *Tzigane*. "It's mostly for Suzanne, but I can put you in at the end." It was fifteen minutes of Suzanne being a gypsy, but then I came on for a great finale, jumping, turning, spinning. "You see, you did very well. I knew you'd do well."

In retrospect, neither of those two ballets was very good, and they were not scheduled again until, years later, I invited Suzanne to stage *Tzigane*. We had had a falling out after she denounced my leadership unfairly in the *New York Times*, and I wanted to make it up by offering her the ballet. "OK, but I make all the casting decisions."

"But Suzanne, I get to make suggestions."

She wouldn't hear of them, especially casting Darci Kistler.

Years before Balanchine had fired Suzanne for making demands. She went to Europe but soon grew unhappy and contacted me, asking to come back. I went to Mr. B and told him.

"Any conditions?" he asked.

"No."

"Bring her back."

Mr. B, however complicated he was, always took care of his dancers, which is something I tried to emulate when I took over the Company, especially when it came to senior dancers.

When I became head of the Company, the first thing I did was ask Betty Cage, the executive director, to show me the finances. I discovered there were many former dancers who were still on the payroll.

"Why are they still being paid?"

"You have to ask Mr. B. It's none of my business."

"But he's dead!"

When I reported this to the Board, I was told to clean it up and made many enemies. "Fuck you!" or "He wanted me to have it," were typical responses. The one thing I insisted upon, however, was that retired members of the Company have health insurance for life. A dancer's life is extremely taxing physically, most careers are relatively short, and the possibility of injury and even lifetime disability is always lurking. When my time to retire came, I insisted upon it again, and, after an unnecessarily extended dispute, I got it.

Figure 111: Photo by Martha Swope shows Martins in *Union Jack*.

• • •

Balanchine was hardly the picture the world knows, of some dictatorial ballet master snapping his whip. In 1977, he choreographed *Union Jack* for me, complete with Scottish reels and a huge cast of 80 on the stage at once. In the sailor section, there was a two-minute solo. He had just finished choreographing the ballet to premiere that night.

"Mr. B, you haven't made my solo yet."

"You make your own solo."

"Are you serious?'

"Yes, I'm tired. I need a drink." It was towards the end of his life.

I did, and it was a huge success. Afterwards, I asked, "How was my solo, Mr. B?"

"Exactly right."

.   .   .

Jerome Robbins was another story. I danced the premiere of *In G Major* by Ravel, which Jerry had choreographed for Suzanne and me. There were a couple of pirouettes in the first movement, and a ten-minute *pas de deux* in the second movement. The audience exploded in applause and wouldn't stop. After the curtain call, Jerry burst into my dressing room without knocking.

"Fuck you! I told you not to overdo the entrance. You did four pirouettes. I only wanted two."

.   .   .

Jerry and Mr. B used to share an office. One day Jerry came to my office and shouted, "You wouldn't believe what that SOB did. He was quoted in the *New York Times* saying, "Whoever choreographed *Les Noces* at American Ballet Theater should burn in Hell."

Jerry also did *Goldberg Variations*, 90 minutes long, with a 45-minute second section. I was warming up when Mr. B came in and held his nose. He hated it.

Not long after, Mr. B came into their shared office. He wouldn't look at Jerry. He fiddled on the piano a bit, then closed it and left.

The Cage, choreographed by Robbins, had a beautiful score by Stravinsky. "It's a terrible ballet," Mr. B said, "You make a new one."

"I can't do that to Jerome Robbins." And he accepted it.

.   .   .

When I was approached about the *Nutcracker* movie, I was very fortunate to be given a lot of authority from the directors of the film, who allowed me editorial rights. I felt they trusted my expertise when it came to dance, and they even expressed gratitude for my involvement.

Darci's debut in *Nutcracker* years earlier was a disaster, so Mr. B insisted, "Next time, she dances it with you." We did dance it together many times, but not for the film. When I look back, Darci's performance as the Sugar Plum Fairy, with Damian Woetzel as her Cavalier, was perhaps her finest performance of *The Nutcracker*.

There were major mishaps, however, including issues with lighting: there were many moments when the spotlight was on Damian and not Darci, which we had to correct in post-production. Another challenge for me was how to address the beginning of the children's angel dance. Unfortunately, I was advised that the way it traditionally begins did not work cinematically, so I had to devise a new beginning. Although a number of dancers requested not to dance certain roles, I was eventually able to persuade them. For example, Wendy Whelan did not want to do the Arabian Dance, but I persuaded her to do it and she was a success.

The movie brought ballet to a much larger audience, elevating dance in the public consciousness and popularizing it. The late director Emile Ardolino did a tremendous job marrying dance and film. When I watch the movie today, I am extraordinarily proud of the product. Of course, that pride is all due to the quality of George Balanchine's production.

. . .

"*Après moi, le Board,*" Mr. B said to me near the end of his life. I guess he wasn't completely sure about me, or the future.

The Board was in awe of Balanchine. The dancers adored him. He was like a god but always a constructive and supportive god. And he could be funny. One time, he was watching from the audience with a microphone when Violette Verdy made a mistake. "Oh, God," she exclaimed.

Over the P.A. system came the reply, "Just call me George."

That is how I remember George Balanchine, and I could tell a thousand more stories about this great man, and what he meant to me, and to twentieth-century ballet.

. . .

When he was in the hospital and the end was drawing near, Mr. B looked at me and said, "Don't be reverent. Be relevant." It was his way of saying that one has to keep moving forward and adapt to changing times. I therefore always tried to focus on the worth of the works and to continue in his spirit. I worked from eight in the morning to ten at night, but never felt burned out. It was what I wanted to do, my calling.

Fig. 112: Photo by Marths Swope pictures Martins and Balanchine together on stage at the New York State Theatre.

Accolades

I had the good fortune to work with many gifted artists and other special colleagues over the decades. Here are some of them and what they have to say about our work together:

Alexey Ratmansky

(b. 1968 Leningrad; Bolshoi Director 2004-8; trained under Pyotr Pestov and Alexandra Markeyeva; principal dancer in Ukrainian National Ballet, Royal Winnepeg and Royal Danish; Artist in residence at ABT 2008; Romeo and Juliet in 20111; 2013 MacArthur Fellow. Alastair Macaulay called him the most gifted choreographer specializing in classical ballet today; in January 2023 NYCB announced he was joining as artist-in-residence in August 2023).

"I first heard about Peter when my teacher showed me Mr. B's *Apollo*; I attended the Choreographic Institute in 2001. Then I did *Russian Seasons* for the Company in 2009. Peter didn't come to the studio but came to rehearsal and was always very positive. When I next did *Concerto in C* at NYCB, the Russian newspapers reprinted my reviews, which was very helpful at that time. When I first saw Peter working, he was like a god. He would take me by the shoulder and give me great support. He continued to grow the Company, avoided re-stagings, and always commissioned new works, creating ballets on the dancers he had, and the dancers were hungry for the steps he gave them. This was partly Mr. B's influence but also Peter's *leadership.* Peter brought along the corps de ballet and advanced them quite quickly, which was unusual in major companies. We had dinner one night and Peter asked me to join him in New York. I asked if I could do a few other things first. He said fine, but then come to us and choreograph. He was very important in my career. He didn't come to the studio if he had confidence in you but somehow knew how things were going. He deserves to be honored in a significant tribute."

Rosemary Dunleavy (Ballet Mistress)

"Peter kept the Company alive after Mr. B died, artistically and financially. Today it's a travesty. Mr. B never said how important Peter was to him, but he showed it. Susie Hendl took the principals as Mistress and I handled the corps. Peter could be demanding and sometimes showed annoyance, which Mr. B never did. Peter was very inventive, brought in artists, architects like Calatrava to design sets, painters, new composers, and contemporary artists like Ray Charles and Wynton Marsalis. His legacy has been marred unfairly. How can you credit an anonymous letter?"

Debbie Koolish (Assistant for 35 years)

"I came from Phoenix in 1964 on a Ford Foundation grant. I retired from dancing early while I was still having a good time, rather than get bitter. I went back a year later as secretary. Peter came to me after I was recommended by Mr. B. Peter is so smart, whatever he didn't know he figured out. He was amazing, paid attention to everything, and had many hidden talents. I also worked for Jerry [Robbins] for a while, but it got to be too much. Peter was fascinated by how everything worked. He studied Mr. B. He created festivals, programs and hired great people. I never saw any sign of misbehavior and worked right next to him, and I never would have stayed if I had. Of course, I could have killed him when he got a DUI! His exoneration by the law firm the board hired to investigate was never made public. Why not? 'Me Too' was a new thing, and after Harvey Weinstein and Charlie Rose, Peter fell victim to it. People resented his charisma and daunting personality. Everyone was drawn to him, like a magnet. A dancer's life is strange. Everyone wants to be promoted, and those who aren't become bitter. One male dancer was the ringleader who spurred on the antics. In the last year, this man came to Peter and cried, saying he had been so wrong. But the board and admin don't want to go there, and don't want to rock the boat. I stayed an extra year after Peter left to handle legal issues and also to be there for the dancers who loved him. His legacy is that he not only succeeded Mr. B, but *triumphed*, artistically and financially."

Gillian Attfield (ex-NYC Ballet Board president)

"Every woman was speechless when Peter came on stage. People got spoiled and entitled. 'You can't tell me what to do.' It's a different age. Dancers have gotten entitled, jealousy enters in. Respect disappears. But his drinking did get in the way. I considered it a private matter. Peter was the star. Once Mr. B was gone, there was never any question but that he would take over. He was a natural leader. It's entertainment, and Peter was a showman. Plus, he built the endowment, and the board supported it and wanted to be part of it. Pieces have to go somewhere. A lot of pieces nowadays don't go anywhere. Those days were fun! Now we have a DEI department. We have to make it full of joy again. Others tried to undermine him, but he was persistent."

Amar Ramasar (recently retired Principal Dancer)

"He was my boss, my teacher, my father. I first came to SAB during Robbins's *Fanfare*. Peter was a great teacher. He could still demonstrate, even in his 60s. He had a commanding presence but was also very human. I was promoted to principal, but with my uptown Bronx, wise-arse attitude, he fired me twice. He yelled at me because I needed it! My father was never in my life, a tough military man, but he finally came to see me in *The Nutcracker*. Backstage Peter took him by the hand, looked deep into his face and asked, "Where have you been? Your son is a star!" And for the first time, my dad broke down and began to cry. Now he's in my life. Criticism for both of us was always one-sided, so I stopped giving interviews, and when I won my case in arbitration, I told him, 'This win is for both of us.' Today I'm a ballet stager and *regisseur* for both the Balanchine and Robbins Trusts, teaching their choreography to todays' dancers. My goal is to transmit the love Peter taught me and pass it onto the next generation."

Megan Fairchild (Principal Dancer from 2005 and author of a self-help book, now getting her MBA):

"I joined NYCB as an apprentice in 2001, became a member of the corps de ballet in 2002, a soloist in 2004, and principal dancer in 2005. I danced the Sugar Plum Fairy [in *The Nutcracker*] in 2011 and *On the Town* on Broadway as Ivy Smith in 2014. When the rumors started, I defended Peter and said I always felt safe working with him. We also did *Apollo, Coppelia* (Swanilda), *Nutcracker, Dewdrop, Marzipan, Harlequinade, Midsummer Nights, Serenade, Symphony in C, Sleeping Beauty,* and *Swan Lake*. Not having him to dance for is like a void. He is a sweet person, and I definitely wanted to please him."

Robbie Fairchild (Principal Dancer from 2005, original Romeo, also starred in Christopher Wheeldon's *American in Paris* on Broadway as Jerry Mulligan. Apprenticed in 2005, soloist 2007, *CATS*, left in 2017 after *Duo Concertant* with Sterling Hyltin)

"The first time he talked to me was about doing *Coppelia* in Saratoga. Everyone else was sick, and he took an interest in me. I had no confidence I could do it, but he took me along. I could never have done it without him. By the time I was 24, I was getting bad reviews and wondered if I should give up. He said, 'My dear, don't change a thing. They don't know your process. You do. Jerry Robbins worried about reviews because he was a theatre man. Mr. B never did.' I have never read a review since. He gave me the freedom to find myself as an artist."

Sterlin Hyltin (came from Amarillo, apprentice in 2002, Soloist in 2006, Principal Dancer in 2007)

"Peter was very kind to me. He made you want to excel. One day he passed me by the elevator and said, 'I always notice you because you always prepare.' It meant so much to me. When you manage ballerinas, you have got to be good at it. Otherwise, they'll eat you alive. I always thought Peter was shy. Some choreographers let you do all the work and then put their name on it. Peter was always very involved. For the *Rose Adagio* in *Sleeping Beauty,* Peter came in late at night and helped me to learn it. The next year he asked me to be his Juliet. Peter loved characters, and he loved acting. He knew how to move the story along, even with a minimal set. One day he came to watch me rehearse *The Nutcracker*, and I could see he was beginning to cry. I followed him afterwards, and he was crying even harder. It was the day after the rumors had begun, and he knew he would soon retire. He was a perfect father figure, and I would defend him until the end. I wrote letters to everyone I could think of and then left the Company. I no longer had the motivation. I love that man."

Perry Silvey (former Production Stage Manager)

"Peter was a great dancer and coach, especially of mime. He had a great eye and talked about dancers and their feet, their energy and costumes, not about their sexuality."

Marguerite Mehler (Production State Manager)

"We all loved Peter and called him 'The Great Dane.' I traveled with him a lot to smaller shows and then to Japan, where I told him I was pregnant. He was always a mentor to us all.

Mark Stanley (Lighting Designer)

"In the American Music Festival, we did 25 new shows in 6 weeks! Peter's relationship to Mr. B was unique as was his relationship to the tradition of story ballet in the 21st century."

Chrisopher Wheeldon OBE (Choreographer)

"I joined the Royal Ballet in 1991 and came to New York in 1993, at the age of 19. I struggled at first to learn the Balanchine Method but was named a soloist in 1998. I began choreographing in 1998 and continued after I retired as a dancer in 2000, after the immense pleasure of doing Jerry Robbins's *Fancy Free*, though sadly after Jerry's death. Peter advised me that I should choose between dancing and choreographing. Sir Kenneth MacMillan had already encouraged me to focus on choreography. Peter had seen something in videos I showed him of my early Royal Ballet choreography and asked me to do something for the SAB Workshop. He was always very interested and supportive but had a knack for politely praising and slightly putting one down simultaneously. Nonetheless, the next year Peter asked me to create something for the larger Choreographic Institute, which was a big deal and very exciting. I have a fond recollection of Peter watching a *Rubies* Rehearsal from the front wing, as Mr. B had usually done. He put his hand on my shoulder and said, 'Look at the corps de ballet and how Mr. B used it so that some are going with the rhythmic pulse of the music, some against, and the principals are doing their own individual steps.' That insight has always stayed with me as I formulated my own choreographies. Peter gave me a huge opportunity by naming me a resident choreographer at New York City Ballet in 2001, and that set me on my future path. Since then, thanks to him, I have created ballets all over the world and also enjoyed success on Broadway. My next big project is next year in Australia, where I will mount a semi-autobiographical Oscar Wilde ballet based mostly on *Dorian Gray* but also incorporating parts of *The Ballad of Reading Gaol.*"

Anna Kisselgoff (former chief dance critic for the *New York Times*):

"Balanchine emphasized speed more than European dance companies, and it took Peter several years to master the Balanchine Method, but he did. Peter never forgot that the essence of ballet is *steps*, not maneuvering. He was one of the great classical dancers of his generation. Under him the NYCB never rejected the ballet vocabulary. When the NYCB went to St. Petersburg, the critics were ecstatic. They said, 'We had been told by Martins's critics that their dancing had deteriorated, but we found the reverse.' Had the dancing deteriorated, they would not have been able to fill the seats for a 21-week season at their very high prices. As it was, they were sold out, and Peter deserves credit for maintaining those standards."

Chapter 11:

Retirement

I retired from dancing in 1983, becoming Co-Ballet Master-In-Chief alongside Jerome Robbins.

Fig. 113: Photo by Steven Caras pictures Robbins, Farrell, Edward I. Koch, and Martins at his farewell performance, 1983.

Fig. 114: Photo by Carolyn George shows Robbins and Martins bowing at Martins' farewell performance.

I ran the Company largely on my own, however, as Jerry had no interest in administration or fundraising. I then became the sole Ballet Master-In-Chief in 1990. I also served as the chairman of faculty of the School of American Ballet, the training division of the New York City Ballet. Those were years of tremendous artistic and financial growth in both institutions. But success, especially in the arts, always brings pushback, and I was no exception. There were always fine critics like Clive Barnes and Anna Kisselgoff who were supportive and fair-minded, but appropriately critical when they thought the occasion demanded it. But such coverage was not unanimous.

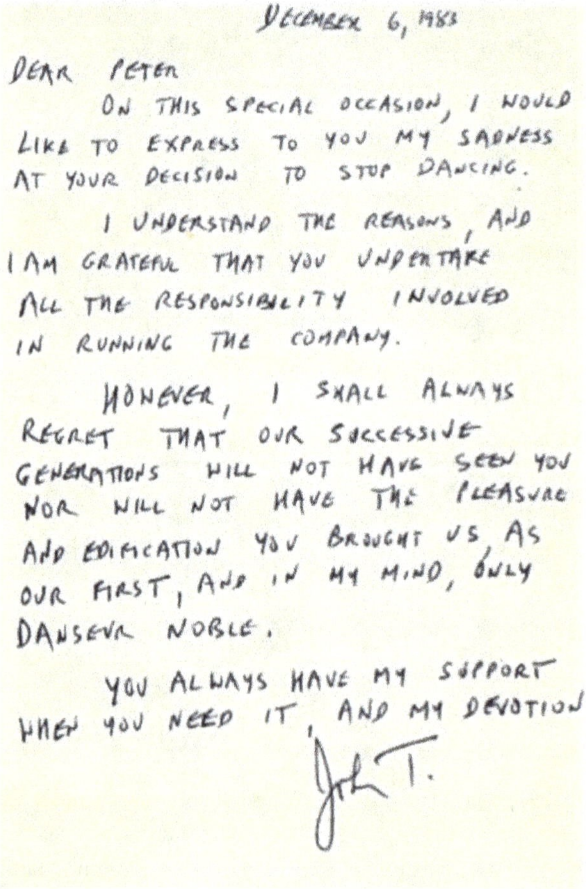

DECEMBER 6, 1983

DEAR PETER

ON THIS SPECIAL OCCASION, I WOULD LIKE TO EXPRESS TO YOU MY SADNESS AT YOUR DECISION TO STOP DANCING.

I UNDERSTAND THE REASONS, AND I AM GRATEFUL THAT YOU UNDERTAKE ALL THE RESPONSIBILITY INVOLVED IN RUNNING THE COMPANY.

HOWEVER, I SHALL ALWAYS REGRET THAT OUR SUCCESSIVE GENERATIONS WILL NOT HAVE SEEN YOU NOR WILL NOT HAVE THE PLEASURE AND EDIFICATION YOU BROUGHT US, AS OUR FIRST, AND IN MY MIND, ONLY DANSEUR NOBLE.

YOU ALWAYS HAVE MY SUPPORT WHEN YOU NEED IT, AND MY DEVOTION

John T.

Fig. 115: John Taras' note to Martins following his retirement in 1983.

Robert Gottlieb was a legendary editor at Alfred A. Knopf and the *New Yorker* who was also a serious balletomane. For some years he served on the board of the New York City Ballet and was characteristically forceful in expressing his opinions.

At different times Mr. B, Lincoln Kirstein and Jerry Robbins all urged me not to deal with Gottlieb. "He's poison," they said. "He doesn't have an objective mind."

Gottlieb was very supportive of me, until Mr. B's death. At that point he did a U-turn and became scathing in his criticisms of my leadership.

Gottlieb would harass me with his ideas and imperious demands at meetings, and even at parties. One day, at his town house in Turtle Bay, he threw out suggestions for programs specifically including Suzanne Farrell, Merrill Ashley, and others.

"Bob," I protested, "This is not the way to make a program. You have to see the bigger picture—periods, colors, music, etc."

But he was relentless and eventually proposed that he be made the NYCB's executive director. "Let me be your Lincoln," he demanded.

One of his writers, Arlene Croce, had also always been very favorably disposed to my work, but upon Mr. B's death she wrote me a letter recommending that I hire a gaggle of downtown people—composers, dancers, choreographers—most of whom were modern dance people, not ballet people. I was not opposed in principle (after all, Mr. B had brought in Martha Graham and Merce Cunningham) so I told Arlene I would consider it. When I did not act on her "suggestions" immediately, however, she became enraged and wrote a diatribe against me that Gottleib published in the *New Yorker*. The next day Gottlieb called my office.

"Hello Bob."

"Did you read Arlene's piece?"

"Yes."

"How did you feel about it?"

"How did you think I felt?"

"Well, in that case, do you want me to resign from the Board? Because I agree with everything she wrote."

Asking Gottlieb to resign could have produced a public squabble that we didn't need, so I just said, "Let's not make any hasty decisions." As it happened, several months later his term would expire, and the more diplomatic path was simply not to renew him. That's what I did, with the Board's support, but forever after Gottlieb considered me an enemy, and, in his dance columns in *The Observer* and his conversations with others, like Alastair Macaulay, was frequently critical of my work. He later worked with Lourdes Lopez in Miami, a spicy and wonderful dancer whom Mr. B had hired as an apprentice when she was 16 and advanced in her career to principal dancer.

This was one of the most unpleasant episodes in my long career. Robert Gottlieb died in the summer of 2023. Recently, Alastair Macaulay wrote me an interesting letter in which he recounted an editing session with Gottlieb on a piece he had written in 1988 on the New York City Ballet's American Music Festival. According to Macaulay, Gottlieb was reviewing his work and suggested that he be more judicious of my merits. I must say that I did often encounter critics who failed to acknowledge my accomplishments, and instead chose only to point out what they believed to be evidence of some kind of mediocrity. I appreciate that Alastair did revise his essay at Gottlieb's request but cannot help but feel that this information came perhaps too little too late.

In his email, Alastair mentioned that Gottlieb, Arlene Croce, and Robert Cornfield often spoke of me over the years, and admitted that, perhaps, it weighed on their conscience that they encouraged my succession but then turned on me. He did not indicate why they did, although he acknowledged that he never knew of Gottlieb's stepping down from the Board at my "behest." In other words, there were many grudges that he was unaware of, and that contributed to, in my opinion, the politics of dance rather than an honest review of my leadership and choreography.

Alastair himself noted that he believed Gottlieb was seeking to take over Lincoln's position, but that he could not be sure. I, however, am sure, and chose to be silent about it in order to protect the Company and Gottlieb himself.

According to Alastair, he believes he and I were perhaps the hardest people for Gottlieb to understand. I agree with him about Gottlieb's competitiveness. Alastair's reviews did indeed, in later years, begin to reflect positive opinions about the Company, and I have no doubt he is telling the truth when he says Gottlieb was unhappy with this. He assured me, however, that Gottlieb eventually conceded. If it was myself and Alastair, as he says, who bothered Gottlieb the most, then I am okay with that.

Nevertheless, Gottlieb apparently did not agree with my departure from the Company as a result of the #MeToo movement and believed I was treated unfairly. While this does not heal the wounds he inflicted on my career, I do give thanks to Macaulay for letting me know, because it does provide some peace of mind. In terms of Alastair, I agree that both of us were lucky that our lives and minds were changed by Balanchine.

The letter from Alastair brought up two memories of Balanchine that I think highlight the complicated relationship between choreographers and critics. One day, Balanchine walked into Company class and asked me if I had read Arlene Croce's scathing review of *Four Temperaments*. Balanchine had re-choreographed the finale of *Four Temperaments*, which was something he had wanted to do ever since its premiere in 1947. He said, "How would she know anything is better now or worse now? She's not a choreographer."

From that moment on, I based my success not on the reviews, but on the pleasure the dancers took in dancing my ballets, and the audience's reception. It was Balanchine who once told me to never forget what newspapers are ultimately for. As he put it, "Wrap your dead fish in them, dear."

•   •   •

After Mr. B's death, the Balanchine Trust was created to administer his ballets and general legacy. Barbara Horgan was retained to run it, and I made sure we kept her on the payroll and provided her with an office so we could keep those ballets close to the NYCB. The ballets produced hundreds of thousands of dollars in royalties each year. "Why should we pay for them?" uninitiated board members would ask. "Didn't he create them especially for us?"

The answer was that Mr. B gave them away to old friends and former wives who needed the income from the licensing fees that we and others paid to present them.

Mr. B gave Lincoln Kirstein *Barocco* and *Orpheus* as a token of his thanks for Kirstein's role in bringing him to America and for their long, if complex, partnership. He left Bizet's *Symphony in C* to Betty Cage, who in turn left it to John Taras. John bequeathed it to me when he died. I did not think it was proper to profit personally from such a bequest, so I donated it to the School of American Ballet, so it could have a badly needed economic cushion. It is arguably Balanchine's single greatest ballet and still performed all over the world. I always did my best to think of the institution's long-term well-being rather than any personal self-interest. When I retired, the Board did not take this into consideration in my settlement, if they even knew about it.

Fig. 116: Photo by Paul Kolnik shows Lincoln Kirstein
on stage with Martins and John Taras toasting Balanchine.

My career at the New York City Ballet was a long and profoundly satisfying run. I wish I could say it ended happily. But in 2017, amidst the growing chorus of the #MeToo Movement, the Company received an anonymous letter accusing me of physical and verbal abuse, dating back a number of years.

I met with two representatives — one from NYCB's Board, and one from SAB's. The Company's legal advisor was also present. They informed me of the anonymous letter. I was told that they would be conducting an investigation into my conduct, which I fully accepted. I did wonder, however, how an anonymous letter should be regarded, both by the organization, and myself. The letter's anonymity made it feel like somewhat of a fishing expedition or witch hunt.

Although I steadfastly deny the truth of these accusations, as well as the despicable and completely false insinuation of sexual abuse that has sometimes been added, including by the *New York Times*, it seemed best for the Company and the School for me to retire, which I did in January 2018. A two-month investigation that preceded my retirement, conducted by independent attorneys, "did not corroborate the allegations of harassment or violence both made in the anonymous letter and reported in the media" regarding me.

I was thus exonerated. But for reasons known best to themselves, the Board members never made this letter public, nor did they voice their support as a body. I must say that I had been feeling that the school needed re-adjustment in its hierarchy for some time. I had proposed that Darci — who had started the young children's program (starting from age 5) — and Jock Soto — who had developed the boy's program — be put in charge of the curriculum. My proposal was vehemently rejected by my co-chair, Kay Mazzo, and by Margie Vandercook, the Executive Director, on the grounds that promoting Darci to that role was a form of nepotism. I found this absurd for multiple reasons: it not only compromised my leadership role, but was an insult to Darci, who had worked at SAB for over 20 years. It was Stanley Williams who asked Darci to begin teaching at SAB as early as 1990, even though she didn't become part of the permanent faculty until 1994. Darci also made a name for herself as a dancer long before we were married in 1991. I no longer felt like I could continue in my role. I was stripped of my authority, and the most qualified teacher at SAB was denied a much deserved promotion. It was after this that I began to consider stepping away from the School, and later the Company.

Still, many Board members have remained close, supportive friends. "When Balanchine died," longtime board member Daniel Shapiro said, "I really thought the New York City Ballet could fold within a couple of years. Instead, Peter brought it to a whole new level. For the board not to support him when the allegations surfaced and were not corroborated in any way was cowardly and terrible. He deserves to be honored." Denise Saul commented, "the way Peter's departure came about was a tragedy. In his 35 years leading it he built the New York City Ballet even beyond what Balanchine had achieved, and if you look around the world, most of the leadership of all the great companies are indebted to Peter."

This was not the end of my difficulties. While I was being investigated in the winter of 2017, I was arrested for a DUI. I went to my local market to buy cigarettes and, because it was January in New York, the conditions were icy and I had snow on my shoes. When I pulled into the parking lot, my foot slid off the brake and hit the accelerator, sending my car into a tree. I panicked, put the car in reverse, and immediately hit another car. When the police arrived, they offered me the choice of taking a breathalyzer test or going to the station. I refused the test because I had been drinking and was taken to the station. I need to note that none of the descriptions above condone my decision to drive that night. I take full responsibility for my actions and am haunted by the possibility that I could have seriously hurt someone. Thankfully, I didn't. Unfortunately, my drinking has affected both my family and my career at times. I would be lying if I said it hasn't. I am ashamed of that and truly sorry to those affected. I hope to reconcile as best I can moving forward.

The day after my DUI, I had a conversation with Charlie Scharf, the Chairman of the Board at NYCB at the time. I told Charlie I had bad news, to which he replied that he did, too. When I reported my being arrested to Charlie, he informed me that some members of the Board already wanted me to step down, and this was the nail in the coffin. I accepted this decision as the best possible path for the School and the Company. We had spoken previously, when the allegations emerged, and I had indicated a willingness to contemplate retirement, not out of guilt, but because of the state of things at SAB, my growing frustrations with both boards, and my desire to save the Company and the School from any further bad press. Obviously, the way it happened was still a crushing experience.

When Darci and I went to my office to pack up my belongings, I received a call from the Executive Director, Kathy Brown, telling me that if I did not complete packing out within the hour, security would remove me. Darci and I went in on a day when we knew the staff and dancers would not be present because I had been notified by the Board and Kathy that they did not want me to be seen by anyone. Darci and I did not encounter anyone other than the security guard, and yet I was nearly forcibly removed from a theater that I danced in for 15 years, ran for 35, and lived most of my life in for 50.

Fig.117: Photo by Martha Swope shows Martins and Balanchine embracing during a rehearsal of *Firebird*.

Fig. 118: Photo by Martha Swope shows Martins choreographing under the tutelage of George Balanchine.

Fig. 119: Photo by Martha Swope pictures Martins bowing following the premier of *Histoire du Soldat*.

Chapter 12:

Legacy

In the summer of 2023, one of my most talented proteges, Joaquín de Luz, invited Darci and me to Madrid, where he is head of the Spanish National Dance Company, to advise on their productions of *Apollo* and Samuel Barber's *Violin Concerto* as part of an "American Program" he had devised. Joaquín had this to say:

> I was born in a small town on the outskirts of Madrid and dreamed of one day dancing at Lincoln Center. I had seen videos of Peter, idolized him and was fortunate enough to get an audition when I went to New York. Afterwards Peter suggested I start at ABT, where I became friends with Peter's son, Nilas. My mom always told me that the biggest risk was not taking one, and after seven years there I told Peter I thought I was now ready. He became my teacher and taught me so much—how to partner (Peter is the best at this in the world). We were both tennis fans and played a lot, though he was a Federer fan and I loved Rafael Nadal. As a joke in rehearsal, one day I even wore a Rafa mask! When I knew I would become a director I told him, and he gave me an invaluable cheat sheet with ideas and suggestions. I waited four seasons to invite him to Madrid until I *knew* the company would be ready for him. Peter and Darci were so generous and modest, and he loved interacting with the company, who in turn were awed by but loved working with him. When I asked him to look at *Apollo*, his first huge success, he looked at me and asked, "You want me to? Really?" And then he plunged in. He was so happy and gave us endlessly positive corrections and suggestions! The company and I are still high from the experience. I have to say it reminded me most unhappily of how unfairly he was treated in the first throes of the #MeToo

accusations, when he was exonerated completely but not really supported by the Board. I remember him crying back during the 2008 financial crisis, when the Board insisted he fire 15 of his dancers, but he did it. And then to be hung out to dry at the end of a brilliant career? It was disgraceful."

Recently, I was asked by a former NYC Ballet Board chair to have lunch with him, the new Board chair, Diana Taylor, and company head, Jonathan Stafford. I accepted on the condition they would consider remounting some of my ballets. There has been a growing perception among dancers and balletomanes that the company needs to find a new footing, and if, at the age of 76, helping advise it on how to do that would be a great privilege.

The New York City Ballet celebrated its 75th anniversary gala in September 2023. I was happy to take part in such a great celebration. The reunion night just before the opening night gala at the Koch Theatre was a joyous gathering with hundreds of our former dancers, many of whom are dear friends. And on January 24, 2024, the Ballet honored me with the first of five performances of Samuel Barber's *Violin Concerto*, one of my favorite choreographic works, and John Adams's *Hallelujah Junction*.

Fig. 120: Photo by Paul Kolnik pictures Darci Kistler and Jock Soto in *Barber's Violin Concerto*.

Figures 121 and 122: Photos by Paul Kolnik picture Darci Kistler
and Jock Soto in *Barber's Violin Concerto* (above) and Meghan Fairchild, Sara
Mearns, Jared Angel, and Charles Askegard in *Barber's Violin Concerto* (below).

Fig. 123: Photo by Paul Kolnik shows Meghan Fairchild
and Charles Askegard in *Barber's Violin Concerto*.

Fig. 124: Photo by Paul Kolnik shows the cast of *Hallelujah Junction*.

Although I was banned from entering the David Koch Theater to rehearse my works for six years, I have now happily returned to rehearse *Violin Concerto* and *Hallelujah Junction*. It has been enormously gratifying to see the latest generation of dancers engage fully and enthusiastically with my choreography. This gives me hope for the future that my relationship with NYCB, particularly with its dancers, is not yet over.

I consider myself most fortunate that the New York City Ballet has been my life's work. Helping it to move forward in a positive direction would not only further enhance my beloved mentor and teacher George Balanchine's legacy, but would also give me the greatest joy.

Darci, whom I married in 1991, has been a generous and loving partner through the best and worst of times. To this day, I can't believe what she has been able to do, teaching at the School of American Ballet, performing, teaching five-year-olds, being a great mother and wife. Often, when our daughter Talicia was little and in school, Darci would commute to New York not once, but twice a day, first to teach and then, in the evening, to perform. She deserves her say, as do my son Nilas and daughter Talicia.

Darci Kistler:

"When I was growing up in Riverside, California, my mother took me to see the NYCB when they came to Los Angeles. We saw the Bolshoi and other companies there as well. Mom subscribed to *Vogue*, and in it I read an article about Mr. B and how he chose a different perfume for each of his dancers, and that intrigued me. I applied and was accepted to SAB in 1976, at the age of twelve. I then came back to New York for two summers and was asked to stay as a permanent student in the Fall. At first, I lived in a Swiss townhouse with other young girls. My mother and grandmother came East to visit me and, one day, as we were walking by Lincoln Center, Mr. B recognized me and walked up to us. "And you must be the mother!," he said, to my grandmother! Needless to say, she fell in love with him instantly. We all did.

I was very fortunate to win an Atlantic Richfield Scholarship, which paid all of my tuition and expenses. Within my first year at the School, I was made an apprentice in the company. I joined the company the following year, began to solo at fifteen, and then at seventeen was named a principal dancer. From early on I sensed Mr. B's love for me and returned it fully. He would do little things, like come into my dressing room to adjust my tiara before a performance so that it was just right. I always felt he was there for me.

I first met Peter dancing at Caramoor in *The Birds*, a ballet choreographed by Ricky Weiss. After the performance, Peter gave me his flowers. Of course, I was attracted to him. Everyone was. We dated on and off, but he had many girlfriends at that stage, and it wasn't serious. My first love was Mr. B. But he saw something in us, and the first time we did *The Nutcracker*, before the performance he put our hands together and said, "I have matched many famous couples in my career, but you will be my favorite couple."

Mr. B singled Peter out about succeeding him but never confirmed that to him. However, he let me know several times that Peter would be taking over the Company when he was gone.

Peter is a great partner. He's very musical and tall and has big hands. He loves dancing with women in front of him, and almost hiding behind ballerinas, so they can shine. He's the opposite of a prima donna, which some male dancers are.

I had injured my ankle tripping on tape that had been laid down on the stage for an orchestral recital at the New York State Theater. At first the doctors said it wasn't broken, but it was. So as Mr. B weakened, I was dealing with that issue and had just broken my ankle rehearsing for the filming of *The Magic Flute*. But one night, I suddenly felt I had to see him and went to the hospital. At first, the receptionist said he could not be seen. I began to cry. I insisted on talking to his nurse. When the nurse came, she said, "He's been asking for you." By the time I got to him, he could no longer speak. But I could tell from his expression and the way he held my hand he knew I was there. I was the last person to see him before he died. To tell the truth, I was shocked by what I saw. I saw fear. He was afraid of dying.

Afterwards I made a long trip to Europe and Peter followed me. He somehow found me in my hotel in Venice, and seven days later I agreed to marry him, so long as there were no other girlfriends. "If we do this," I told him, "I'm in it for the long haul." I have always prided myself on my work ethic and being a professional. I've always felt that I had enough love for others, and that it would never give out. It's because of Mr. B. that I have stayed with Peter. The kind of love and respect he gave and instilled in us, that never goes away.

But Peter is also a very complex person, often concealing his emotions behind a poker face. The way his career ended was terrible, but he tried not to let it show. He felt tremendous pain inside and drank too much. His driving home at night used to terrify me in that period, because I was desperately afraid that he would hurt himself or others.

The 75th Anniversary Reunion was such a wonderful, warm occasion, and it was profoundly moving to see so many friends and former colleagues, including students of mine from the children's program I came up with at the School of American Ballet.

As much as I loved my ballet career, I can move on and enjoy other pursuits. Peter is still focused on the dance world and coaching. Lourdes Lopez has invited him to Miami to help coach the principal dancers in Mr. B's production of *A Midsummer Night's Dream*. Talicia and I want to buy a camper and visit our national parks. I want to take Peter to Africa, where I visited decades ago and he has never been. There are infinite opportunities on the horizon, and I look forward to them all."

.   .   .

Recently, Darci and I went to Howard Solomon's memorial at the New York Historical Society. His son Andrew had battled depression, and Howard's company, Forrest Laboratories, developed Zoloft to treat it, which proved to be a miracle drug. Howard was a great patron of opera and dance, but on a video they showed he said his true legacy was family. It made me think again of Mr. B's warning against marriage. Ultimately, though, his last words to me were that "Family is the most important thing."

Driving home Darci asked, "Honey, what is your legacy?"

I wish I could say I was a great husband and father, but the truth is I wasn't. I wish I could rewrite that script. For example, I often clashed with my son, Nilas, mainly over work. Once I had to pull him out of a performance after he had gained too much weight over the summer, and he was furious. Another time I turned down his request that his wife dance *Swan Lake* and he wouldn't speak to me for months. But today we have become closer than we have ever been.

Fig. 125: Family portrait of Peter Martins and his son, Nilas Martins.

Nilas Martins:

"From the ages of four to eleven, I went from Denmark to Saratoga Springs for three weeks to be with my dad during the SPAC season. If he was working or performing, I was babysat by members of the company. I then went to the School of American Ballet and joined the company. The ballet masters were my boss, and dad let me be. We would be together a lot, and play tennis at his house, which we both loved, but then it was time to get down to business, and I knew I had to put my best foot forward. He never overcoached me but let me develop my own style. He has always had an amazing work ethic, and his own ballets are very taxing physically. But I always knew he was there, and he knew I could come to him if I needed to."

Fig. 126: Photo by Martha Swope of Nilas Martins in *Fool for You*.

My daughter Talicia has this to say:

Talicia Martins

"Growing up, my whole identity was Mom and Dad, but not in the sense people might think. To me, my parents were imperfect, admirable, complicated, sometimes distant from me while being wholly connected to others. I never saw them as stars, even though they were. They were to me only Mom and Dad, who happened to be supremely successful. Perhaps because I was their child, it took years to appreciate the scope of what they had achieved. It wasn't until I got older that I began to realize why so many people asked Peter for photos or autographs, or why strange old people at galas told me I was so lucky to be his daughter. Today, I can say that I am proud of everything he accomplished while at New York City Ballet, even if it is harder to come to terms with the state of our personal relationship as daughter and father.

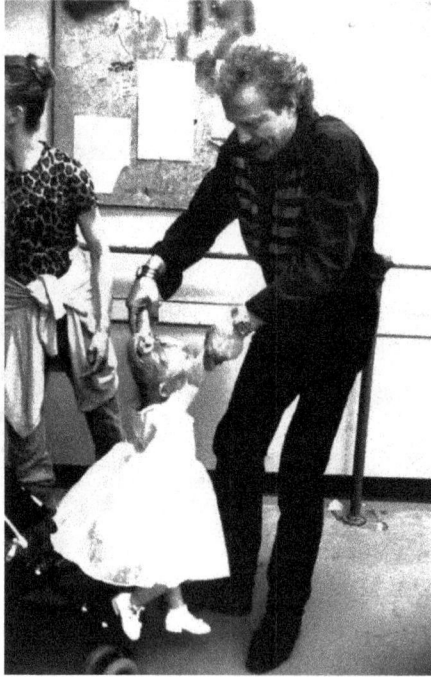

Figures 127 and 128: Family portraits of Martins, Kistler, and Talicia in the Main Hall at New York City Ballet.

I spent a lot of time alone as a child. I was simply a lonely kid. In a sense I was raised with the company, attending rehearsals and performances from a young age. I danced for a while, but knew I could never live up to them, so now I've headed quite happily towards the law.

I can tell you one thing: Peter worked constantly. He was always up at 4:30 in the morning. He would study the programs, wait for the *New York Times* to arrive, and then read it in its entirety. He would drive me to school, and then I wouldn't see him again until he came home around midnight, when Mom would cook dinner for us. I never got any sleep. Still, I wouldn't trade any of it. I have such wonderful memories of New York City Ballet. It was my home for most of my life, the dancers were my family and friends, and the staff were my babysitters, so to speak. It was Debbie who watched me while Peter was in meetings, and it was Albert Evans who, to me, felt like a godfather. I would put on my Mom's pointe shoes — that were way too big for me — and attempt to dance in the principal dressing room in Saratoga, despite actual dancers attempting to get ready for performance. For the most part, the company was truly my family, and it was a family cultivated by my dad, and also my mom. She deserves so much credit. The saying is cheesy and overused, but I truly believe that behind every great man is an even greater woman. When mom retired, I think I was more heartbroken than anyone else. The last year of her dancing I insisted that I watch every one of her performances.

It was years later that Peter suggested he was ready to retire. I must say, I was shocked. We were having dinner alone at L'Inizio, in Ardsley, New York, in late 2016, before the accusations surfaced the following year. Dinners alone with my dad didn't happen often and, to be honest, I was shocked that he confided in me. To this day, it is likely my most cherished memory with him.

That night, Peter said to me, "Can I tell you something I haven't told anyone? I'm ready to retire. I don't think I want to renew my contract." And then he broke down and cried. My father, for the first time that I could remember, told me he was tired, discouraged, and broken. Ironically, I was also tired, discouraged, and broken, and perhaps he sensed that. As many people know I have made severe mistakes in my life, hurting both myself and others, but his vulnerability that night, and his willingness to share, paved the way for my own journey towards self-reflection and healing. In watching Peter's work ethic, and his ability to cope with the loss of his career, family at NYCB, and, in many ways, his reputation, I gained the strength and guidance to confront those same issues in my own life. I will always be inspired by the dedication he put into the company, and have come to accept that NYCB, particularly Mr. B, means more to him than anything in the world.

· · ·

Growing up in Denmark, I was not a great student. My sisters used to ridicule me, calling me stupid and playing mean tricks like making me a sandwich that only had soap in it. My only strong subjects were English and geography. To this day, I can name every American state and its capital, but what use is that really? However, I do take great satisfaction that my children are both bright, and of course Darci deserves credit for much of that.

I want to close this memoir by returning to its central subject, George Balanchine. He was a genius, but a modest man, and few people have ever understood or commented on what made him one. He himself said, "I never invented anything; I just assemble." Another time he said, "If I invented anything it was the break-up of the musical meter." By this he meant that choreographers up until his time had followed the example of the great Marius Petipa, whose choreography mimicked the musical score, whereas Balanchine choreographed *against* it. For example, if the music was written in 4, Balanchine would choreograph in 5; if the music was written in 8, Mr. B would choreograph in 7. That kept it interesting! In *The Nutcracker's* last variation, the Sugar Plum Fairy's diagonal is choreographed in 7, not 8. There was thus always a tension between the music and the dancing, which made it more exciting than traditional choreography.

Contemporary choreographers attuned to classical ballet are keenly aware of Mr. B's landmark innovation and appreciate it, because it is so ingenious, yet also so subtle. Everything Petipa did was, "One *and*," and it was down on the "and," whereas with Balanchine the down was on the *one*. "Down on the one" was not so much an innovation as it was an aesthetic choice, but the excitement it lent his ballets made the difference between them being merely good and being truly great. This was evident as early as in parts of *Apollo,* which Balanchine choreographed in 1928, when he himself was only 24, but it became more fully fledged in his work as his career progressed. And it's what makes his ballets still fresh and unpredictable today.

I had the privilege of observing this for over 35 years in dozens of Balanchine's ballets, and freely admit to having stolen from him at times, but I have never read one critic who mentioned this fundamental aspect of Balanchine's art. No one, not even Clive Barnes nor Alastair Macaulay, ever wrote about it, nor have other dancers who wrote about dance. And yet this is his greatest innovation.

Balanchine's true greatness lies here and is what makes his ballets still so vital and relevant today.

George Balanchine was my savior. He gave me my mission in life and was the wisest man I have ever known. So, to answer Darci's question, probably my greatest legacy is my contribution to ballet as a dancer, choreographer, and caretaker of Mr. B's legacy. Following his lead, and in his honor, I have always tried my best to be relevant, not reverent. And I'm satisfied with that.

Fig. 129: Photo by Martha Swope pictures Peter Martins waving goodbye (to ballet) in his famous role in *Apollo.*

Appendix:

Peter Martins's Company Biography

Peter Martins was the Ballet Master in Chief of New York City Ballet for 35 years, making him the only person to preside over the Company as long as its founder, George Balanchine. Martins, born in Denmark, began his association with NYCB in 1967, when he was invited to dance the title role in George Balanchine's *Apollo*, during the Company's appearance at the Edinburgh Festival. He then performed as a guest artist with NYCB for three years before joining the Company as a principal dancer in 1970. Prior to retiring from dancing in 1983, Martins danced a tremendous variety of roles with the Company and was lauded for his outstanding partnering skills and noble stage presence.

In 1981, Martins was named Ballet Master for the New York City Ballet, a title he shared with George Balanchine, Jerome Robbins, and John Taras. From 1983 to 1989, Martins served as Co-Ballet Master in Chief with Jerome Robbins, although Mr. Martins ran the day-to-day operations. He assumed sole directorship of the Company in 1990. In addition, Martins became Chairman of the Faculty of the School of American Ballet, the official school of NYCB. He then went on to found the New York Choreographic Institute, and assume the position of Director.

Martins began his career as a choreographer in 1977 with *Calcium Light Night*, set to several pieces of music by Charles Ives. He has since created nearly 90 ballets – primarily for NYCB – ranging from *pas de deux* to large-scale pieces, set to music by composers as diverse as Tchaikovsky and Stravinsky, Wynton Marsalis, and John Adams. His full-length productions for New York City Ballet include *The Sleeping Beauty* (1991), *Swan Lake* (1999), *Romeo + Juliet* (2007), and *La Sylphide* (2015).

During his tenure as Ballet Master in Chief, Martins directed several important festivals and anniversary celebrations. In 1988, to celebrate the Company's 40th anniversary, he conceived the American Music Festival, a three-week celebration of American music, art, and dance. In 1993, on the occasion of the tenth anniversary of Balanchine's death, Mr. Martins planned the Company's historic Balanchine Celebration, which featured a season-long retrospective of Balanchine's work performed in chronological order. In 1998, Martins planned the 50th Anniversary Season, a year-long celebration featuring an unprecedented performance schedule of more than 100 ballets during the Company's winter and spring seasons. For the Company's 2003-2004 season, to commemorate the 100th Anniversary of the birth of George Balanchine, Martins conceived *Balanchine 100: The Centennial Celebration,* as a year-long exhibition-style approach to Balanchine's life and work. In 2008, the Company presented the Robbins Celebration, honoring the 90th anniversary of the choreographer's birth.

During the 2010 spring season Martins conceived NYCB's landmark *Architecture of Dance – New Choreography and New Music Festival* which featured seven world premiere ballets, four commissioned scores, and sets designed by acclaimed architect Santiago Calatrava. For NYCB's 2017 Spring Season, Martins programmed a historic look at choreography created for New York City Ballet since 1988. Called *Here/Now,* the festival featured 43 ballets by 22 different choreographers.

In September 2000, Martins and the late philanthropist Irene Diamond launched the New York Choreographic Institute. Each year, the Institute provides selected choreographers with the opportunity to work with NYCB dancers in the Company's rehearsal studios at Lincoln Center. These sessions give choreographers a rare chance to explore and experiment, without the pressures of preparing for a performance.

Martins's autobiography, *Far From Denmark,* was published by Little, Brown in 1982. In addition to having received numerous other awards, in 2008 Mr. Martins was made a Commander in the Order of Arts and Letter by the government of France. In his native Denmark, Mr. Martins was made a Knight of Dannebrog by Queen Margrethe II in September 1983. He was subsequently named a Knight of the First Order and, in April 2013, a Commander of the Knights of Dannebrog, which is Denmark's highest civilian honor. In 2008, Mr. Martins was inducted into the National Museum of Dance Hall of Fame, in Saratoga Springs, New York.

Figures Index

Fig. 1: © *Paul Kolnik, all rights reserved.*

Fig. 2: *Jerome Robbins Dance Division, The New York Public Library for the Performing Arts.*

Fig. 3: *Jerome Robbins Dance Division, The New York Public Library for the Performing Arts.*

Fig. 4: *Photo by Rigmor Mydtskov © Jerome Robbins Dance Division, The New York Public Library for the Performing Arts*

Fig. 7: The letter reads, "As announced to you last year, when your son Peter was admitted to Balletelevskolen, the children's standback will be discussed in depth several times a year. After the end of the ballet school year and the thus held the exam the other day for the school's teachers of censors, I would like to inform them that there is a strong doubt about Peter's suitability for the ballet. However, the time is seen to discuss the question again over the coming season".

Fig. 8: *Photo by Martha Swope ©Jerome Robbins Dance Division, The New York Public Library for the Performing Arts*

Fig. 9: *Photo by Martha Swope ©Jerome Robbins Dance Division, The New York Public Library for the Performing Arts*

Fig. 10: *Jerome Robbins Dance Division, The New York Public Library for the Performing Arts.*

Fig. 11: *Jerome Robbins Dance Division, The New York Public Library for the Performing Arts.*

Fig. 12: *Photo by Martha Swope ©Jerome Robbins Dance Division, The New York Public Library for the Performing Arts.*
Balanchine is a trademark of The George Balanchine Trust.
The Nutcracker
Choreography by George Balanchine
© The George Balanchine Trust

Fig. 13: *Jerome Robbins Dance Division, The New York Public Library for the Performing Arts.*
Balanchine is a trademark of The George Balanchine Trust.
Apollo

Violin Concerto
Choreography by George Balanchine
© The George Balanchine Trust

Fig. 25: © *Steven Caras, all rights reserved.*

Fig. 26: © *Steven Caras, all rights reserved.*

Fig. 27: © *Steven Caras, all rights reserved.*
Balanchine is a trademark of The George Balanchine Trust.
Tzigane
Choreography by George Balanchine
© The George Balanchine Trust

Fig. 28: *Jerome Robbins Dance Division, The New York Public Library for the Performing Arts.*
Balanchine is a trademark of The George Balanchine Trust.
Chaconne
Choreography by George Balanchine
© The George Balanchine Trust

Fig. 29: © *Steven Caras, all rights reserved.*
Balanchine is a trademark of The George Balanchine Trust.
Diamonds
Choreography by George Balanchine
© The George Balanchine Trust

Fig. 30: *Photo by Martha Swope ©Jerome Robbins Dance Division, The New York Public Library for the Performing Arts.*
Balanchine is a trademark of The George Balanchine Trust.
Chaconne
Choreography by George Balanchine
© The George Balanchine Trust

Fig. 31: *Photo by Martha Swope ©Jerome Robbins Dance Division, The New York Public Library for the Performing Arts.*
Balanchine is a trademark of The George Balanchine Trust.
Chaconne
Choreography by George Balanchine
© The George Balanchine Trust

Fig. 32: *Photo by Martha Swope ©Jerome Robbins Dance Division, The New York Public Library for the Performing Arts.*

Fig. 33: *Photo by Martha Swope ©Jerome Robbins Dance Division, The New York Public Library for the Performing Arts.*

Fig. 34: © *Carolyn George, all rights reserved.*
Balanchine is a trademark of The George Balanchine Trust.
Brahms–Schoenberg

Fig. 96: *Photo by Martha Swope ©Jerome Robbins Dance Division, The New York Public Library for the Performing Arts.*
Balanchine is a trademark of The George Balanchine Trust.
Tzigane
Choreography by George Balanchine
© The George Balanchine Trust

Fig. 99: *Photo by Martha Swope ©Jerome Robbins Dance Division, The New York Public Library for the Performing Arts.*

Fig. 100: © *Estate of Roy Lichtenstein, 1988.*

Fig. 102: *Photo by Martha Swope ©Jerome Robbins Dance Division, The New York Public Library for the Performing Arts.*
Balanchine is a trademark of The George Balanchine Trust.
Coppelia
Choreography by George Balanchine
© The George Balanchine Trust

Fig. 103: © *Steven Caras, all rights reserved.*
Balanchine is a trademark of The George Balanchine Trust.
Coppelia
Choreography by George Balanchine
© The George Balanchine Trust

Fig. 104: © *Steven Caras, all rights reserved.*
Balanchine is a trademark of The George Balanchine Trust.
Orpheus
Choreography by George Balanchine
© The George Balanchine Trust

Fig. 105: © *Steven Caras, all rights reserved.*

Fig. 106: © *Paul Kolnik, all rights reserved.*
Balanchine is a trademark of The George Balanchine Trust.
Davidsbündlertänze
Choreography by George Balanchine
© The George Balanchine Trust

Fig. 107: *Photo by Martha Swope ©Jerome Robbins Dance Division, The New York Public Library for the Performing Arts.*
Balanchine is a trademark of The George Balanchine Trust.
Davidsbündlertänze
Choreography by George Balanchine
© The George Balanchine Trust

Fig. 108: © *Steven Caras, all rights reserved.*

Fig. 109: © *Steven Caras, all rights reserved.*

Fig. 110: *© Steven Caras, all rights reserved.*

Fig. 111: *Photo by Martha Swope ©Jerome Robbins Dance Division, The New York Public Library for the Performing Arts.*

Fig. 112: *Photo by Martha Swope ©Jerome Robbins Dance Division, The New York Public Library for the Performing Arts.*

Fig. 113: *© Steven Caras, all rights reserved.*

Fig. 114: *© Carolyn George, all rights reserved.*

Fig. 116: *© Paul Kolnik, all rights reserved.*

Fig. 117: *Photo by Martha Swope ©Jerome Robbins Dance Division, The New York Public Library for the Performing Arts.*

Fig. 118: *Photo by Martha Swope ©Jerome Robbins Dance Division, The New York Public Library for the Performing Arts.*

Honors and Awards
Presented to Peter Martins

2016
Remise de la Grande Médaille de Vermeil

2008
Inducted into the National Museum of Dance, Hall of Fame in Saratoga Springs
Appointed Commander of the Order of Arts and Letters in France
William Shakespeare Award for Classical Theatre

2003
Harbor Salute to Achievement (Boys and Girls Harbor)

2001
Americans for the Arts Artistic Leadership Award

2000
New York State Council on the Arts Governor's Arts Award
Career Transition for Dancers Award for Outstanding Contribution to the World of Dance

1998
Arts & Business Council Kitty Carlisle Hart Award

1997
Promoted to Knight of The Order of Dannebrog in the First Degree
"Benois" de la Danse Award

1996
Appointed to Officer of the Order of Arts and Letters in France

1994
American-Scandinavian Foundation Cultural Award

1991

Eleanor Lambert Ltd.'s International Best Dressed List

1990

American Academy of Achievement's "The Golden Plate" Award

1989

La Médaille de la Ville de Paris

1986

Anglo-American Contemporary Dance Foundation "Astaire Award" for Choreography of *Song and Dance*

Monitor Award Finalist for Best Director in Local Commercials for "Tour 1985"

Renewed term as Associate Fellow of Yale University's Calhoun College

1985

League of American Theatres and Producers Antoinette Perry Nomination in Outstanding Choreography for *Song and Dance*

Drama Desk Nomination in Outstanding Choreography for *Song and Dance*

1984

Dance Masters of America Award

Philadelphia Art Alliance Award of Merit

1983

Designated Knight of The Order of Dannebrog by Queen Margrethe II of Denmark

Academy of Television Arts & Sciences Nomination for Outstanding Achievement in Choreography for a Single Episode of a Regular or Limited Series or for a Special for *A Choreographer's Notebook: Stravinsky Piano Ballets by Peter Martins*

Barnard College Arts In the City Award

1982

Drama Desk Award Nomination in the Category of Outstanding Choreography for *On Your Toes*

1981

New York City Commission for Cultural Affairs Mayor's Award of Honor for Art & Culture

Appointed Associate Fellow (five-year term) at Yale University's Calhoun College

1980

Danish American Society 1980 Man-of-the-Year Award

1979

Dance Educators of America Award

Harkness Dance Award

1978

Nijinsky Prize

1977

Dance Magazine Award

Cue Magazine Golden Apple Award

Acknowledgments

I am grateful for the support of the Hon. Earle Mack, perhaps my oldest friend, and Gillian Attfield, for her unequaled support of me throughout my tenure. Without their contributions, this book would not have been possible. I am equally grateful for the assistance of Jamie MacGuire, and for Paul du Quenoy's conviction that my story needed to be told. I am equally grateful to all of those who were willing to give accolades on my behalf, in particular Debbie Koolish, who was not only my assistant and dear friend for 35 years but who managed to put up with me during that time. I want to thank my wife, Darci, without whom my career, legacy, and family would not be possible. In addition, I want to thank my children for their support and, in particular, Talicia, who played a huge role in writing this book. I also must acknowledge Stanley Williams, who was perhaps the greatest ballet instructor anywhere in the world. Lastly, and above all else, I want to acknowledge George Balanchine for simply being Mr. B.

Fig. 130: Family photo of Earle Mack, Carol Mack,
Nilas Martins, Darci Kistler, and Peter Martins.

www.ingramcontent.com/pod-product-compliance
Lightning Source LLC
Chambersburg PA
CBHW060417100426
42812CB00037B/3491/J